Task Intelligence for
Search and Recommendation

Synthesis Lectures on Information Concepts, Retrieval, and Services

Editor

Gary Marchionini, *University of North Carolina, Chapel Hill*

Synthesis Lectures on Information Concepts, Retrieval, and Services publishes short books on topics pertaining to information science and applications of technology to information discovery, production, distribution, and management. Potential topics include: data models, indexing theory and algorithms, classification, information architecture, information economics, privacy and identity, scholarly communication, bibliometrics and webometrics, personal information management, human information behavior, digital libraries, archives and preservation, cultural informatics, information retrieval evaluation, data fusion, relevance feedback, recommendation systems, question answering, natural language processing for retrieval, text summarization, multimedia retrieval, multilingual retrieval, and exploratory search.

Digital Libraries for Cultural Heritage: Development, Outcomes, and Challenges from European Perspectives
Tatjana Aparac-Jelšić
2017

iRODS Primer 2: Integrated Rule-Oriented Data System
Hao Xu, Terrell Russell, Jason Coposky, Arcot Rajasekar, Reagan Moore, Antoine de Torcy, Michael Wan, Wayne Shroeder, and Sheau-Yen Chen
2017

Information Architecture: The Design and Integration of Information Spaces, Second Edition
Wei Ding, Xia Lin, and Michael Zarro
2017

Fuzzy Information Retrieval
Donald H. Kraft and Erin Colvin
2017

Quantifying Research Integrity
Michael Seadle
2016

Incidental Exposure to Online News
Borchuluun Yadamsuren and Sanda Erdelez
2016

Web Indicators for Research Evaluation: A Practical Guide
Michael Thelwall
2016

Trustworthy Policies for Distributed Repositories
Reagan W. Moore, Hao Xu, Mike Conway, Arcot Rajasekar, Jon Crabtree, and Helen Tibbo
2016

The Notion of Relevance in Information Science: Everybody knows what relevance is. But, what is it really?
Tefko Saracevic
2016

Dynamic Information Retrieval Modeling
Grace Hui Yang, Marc Sloan, and Jun Wang
2016

Learning from Multiple Social Networks
Liqiang Nie, Xuemeng Song, and Tat-Seng Chua
2016

Task Intelligence for Search and Recommendation
Chirag Shah and Ryen W. White

ISBN: 978-3-031-01198-6   paperback
ISBN: 978-3-031-02326-2   ebook
ISBN: 978-3-031-00233-5   hardcover

DOI 10.1007/978-3-031-00233-5

A Publication in the Springer series
SYNTHESIS LECTURES ON INFORMATION CONCEPTS, RETRIEVAL, AND SERVICES

Lecture #74
Series Editor: Gary Marchionini, *University of North Carolina, Chapel Hill*
Series ISSN
Print 1947-945X   Electronic 1947-9468

Task Intelligence for Search and Recommendation

Chirag Shah
University of Washington

Ryen W. White
Microsoft Research

SYNTHESIS LECTURES ON INFORMATION CONCEPTS, RETRIEVAL, AND SERVICES #74

ABSTRACT

While great strides have been made in the field of search and recommendation, there are still challenges and opportunities to address information access issues that involve solving tasks and accomplishing goals for a wide variety of users. Specifically, we lack intelligent systems that can detect not only the request an individual is making (what), but also understand and utilize the intention (why) and strategies (how) while providing information and enabling task completion. Many scholars in the fields of information retrieval, recommender systems, productivity (especially in task management and time management), and artificial intelligence have recognized the importance of extracting and understanding people's tasks and the intentions behind performing those tasks in order to serve them better. However, we are still struggling to support them in task completion, e.g., in search and assistance, and it has been challenging to move beyond single-query or single-turn interactions. The proliferation of intelligent agents has unlocked new modalities for interacting with information, but these agents will need to be able to work understanding current and future contexts and assist users at task level. This book will focus on *task intelligence* in the context of search and recommendation. Chapter 1 introduces readers to the issues of detecting, understanding, and using task and task-related information in an information episode (with or without active searching). This is followed by presenting several prominent ideas and frameworks about how tasks are conceptualized and represented in Chapter 2. In Chapter 3, the narrative moves to showing how task type relates to user behaviors and search intentions. A task can be explicitly expressed in some cases, such as in a to-do application, but often it is unexpressed. Chapter 4 covers these two scenarios with several related works and case studies. Chapter 5 shows how task knowledge and task models can contribute to addressing emerging retrieval and recommendation problems. Chapter 6 covers evaluation methodologies and metrics for task-based systems, with relevant case studies to demonstrate their uses. Finally, the book concludes in Chapter 7, with ideas for future directions in this important research area.

KEYWORDS

tasks, task intelligence, search, information seeking and retrieval, recommendation, evaluation

Contents

Preface

Tasks are a driving force behind interactions with search and recommendation systems. Task-based intelligent systems can assist users in a variety of ways, including generating search results, presenting contextual reminders, organizing to-do tasks, scheduling time for tasks, and supporting task completion directly, e.g., in task-oriented dialog systems. Task is often regarded as a latent factor in interactions with these systems and users are frequently unassisted in managing tasks across query, session, application, and device boundaries.

There have been many research studies on tasks, spanning the information retrieval (IR), recommender systems, and human–computer interaction (HCI) research communities, among others, including several by the two of us. There have also been several well-attended workshops and tracks at venues such as the Text REtrieval Conference (TREC), designed to build community and drive progress in this area. However, there has been no real attempt to bring together much of the relevant work in a single place, especially as it relates to IR.

We wanted to write a book to address this shortcoming and help the community grasp the extent of the significant opportunity in task-based search and recommendation. We also wanted to present our point of view on the challenges and opportunities in this area. This book builds on our SIGIR 2020 tutorial of the same name, providing additional commentary and detail to augment the slides and the oral presentation. These narratives are built on the shoulders of many past and present scholars in the field. We have done our best to honor and introduce their ideas in the context pertinent to this book. In addition, we have taken co-authored works with our collaborators and students for several of the case studies described here. This list of scholars include Nicholas Belkin, Jiqun Liu, Matthew Mitsui, Shawon Sarkar, and Yiwei Wang. Presenting their work in the context of this book and its narrative warranted some repetitions or re-narrations, but the reader is encouraged to read those original works and cite them appropriately.

As outlined in the Abstract, the book is organized in seven chapters with what we believed to be a logical structure. Each reader can decide where they should start and how deep they should go into the provided material. In case of no prior exposure to this topic, one should certainly start with Chapter 1. Those who already have some familiarity with this area can choose to review Chapters 2 and 3 to ensure they are not missing any important or recent works and then move to a more careful examination of the chapters that follow. Seasoned scholars in the field may want to jump straight to several case studies presented in Chapters 3–5 and round it out with special emphasis on evaluation in Chapter 6. Almost everyone, regardless of their background, should consider reviewing and reflecting on Chapter 7.

No matter what your background is and how much you intend to work in this area, we hope that you find the content helpful and that it inspires you and your colleagues to do more work on this important topic.

Chirag Shah and Ryen W. White
May 2021

Acknowledgments

We are grateful to our families for their constant love and support; for our colleagues, collaborators, and students for their contributions to our scholarship; and our critics and reviewers for helping us question that which we may take for resolved.

Chirag Shah and Ryen W. White
May 2021

CHAPTER 1

Introduction

"A wealth of information creates a poverty of attention."—this statement by renowned economist and psychologist Herbert A. Simon in 1971 is perhaps even more fitting today as we are drenched in the sea of information on one hand, but lack tools and support for going beyond retrieving relevant information and meet higher level goals of solving problems and making decisions on the other. This applies to most of our information systems, specifically search and recommendation systems. These systems are often optimized for matching a situation, a need, or an expression of a need (query, question) to available information. However, they do little to consider the task behind those needs and situations. Invariably, their underlying assumption is that fulfilling a user's request one at a time would also address their overall task.

In this chapter, we will argue that this assumption is flawed and that understanding the task that motivates someone to seek information is critical for going beyond just finding relevant information and making information help us solve problems. This is not a new realization, as we will see in the following section. We will then provide examples and scenarios to demonstrate how considering task information could be critical in helping people with their informational needs. And finally, we will provide the outline of what this book will do and how.

1.1 WHAT IS A TASK?

IR systems, whether they are manifested as everyday search (e.g., in search engines such as Google and Bing) or special tools for providing interventions and recommendations (e.g., digital assistants such as Alexa and e-commerce sites such as Amazon.com), cover a rather significant component of advanced intelligent assistance. For simplicity, we refer to these broadly as IR systems. People's interactions with these systems are often motivated by tasks that emerge from evolving, continuous problematic situations [31, 32]. Understanding a searcher's intention and task for asking a question could provide an effective method for conceptualizing different contexts and situations of information needs that drive people to seek information using different information systems. Search and retrieval systems have evolved considerably over the last few decades; they have become more advanced in suggesting useful queries, and providing personalized search results, especially in fact-finding and navigational search tasks [332]. However, their algorithmic processes are still limited while retrieving information supporting complex and intellectually challenging tasks [115]. Often, current information systems fail to provide information relevant to achieve searchers' complex task goals, or are unable to suggest useful queries to exclude or execute next, in order to retrieve Web pages containing useful information for

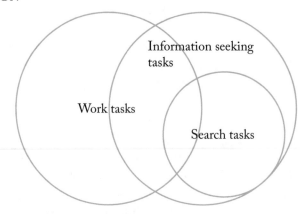

Figure 1.1: Conceptualization of task in search situations.

searchers' tasks. Even though scholars have long argued the importance of considering task information in IR for truly helping people with complex, unexpressed, or unclear needs [28, 85], incorporating tasks in IR systems has been challenging at best. However, there are several bright spots and certainly research that can help us move further. In this book, we will review many such efforts and discuss what they mean for task-based intelligent search and recommendation systems. Before that, let us discuss how we think about *task* as a general and IR-specific concept.

A task is generally considered as a set of connected physical, affective, and cognitive actions through which individuals try to accomplish some goals in their work or everyday lives [51, 312]. It is an expression or representation of the *goal* or *purpose* of the search process (e.g., "gathering information to write a research report" or "planning a trip") [146]. A task can also be interpreted as an atomic information need from a more granular perspective resulting in one or more queries submitted to IR systems [138]. Finally, according to existing empirical research, a task can be inherently hierarchical, multidimensional, and modeled at multiple granularity levels [52, 53].

In general, a task consists of three levels: work task, information seeking task, and search or retrieval task (see Figure 1.1), each with its own goals, intentions, conditions, actions, and outcomes [52]. At its most general level, work task refers to the broad, overarching goal which triggers the search process. That overarching task consists of one or more information seeking tasks, which could be accomplished through multiple consultations with one or more information sources such as search systems and human experts. Each seeking task can then be further deconstructed to one or more information retrieval/search tasks with a defined goal but an anticipated and likely unknown outcome [307] that can be accomplished through a single consultation with search systems [53, 210, 354]. Each level of the search task can be modeled as a concrete sequence of states and actions. Each level of task has a defined goal but an anticipated and likely unknown outcome [307]. Furthermore, each sub-task level is recursively dependent on previous one(s) [210]. Under the influence of local situational aspects of search, users' task states at a given moment of a search process often change and evolve during search interactions [195].

1.2   REASONS TO CONSIDER TASK IN IR

While great strides have been made in the field of search and recommendation, there are still challenges and opportunities to address information access issues that involve solving tasks and accomplishing goals for a wide variety of users. Specifically, we lack intelligent systems that can detect not only the request an individual is making (what), but also understand and utilize the intention (why) and strategies (how) while providing information.

This is not a new realization or an argument. Many scholars in IR and beyond have recognized the importance of extracting and understanding a user's task and the underlying intention in order to serve them better [226, 235, 311].

Despite such support for understanding and using task knowledge, we are still struggling to move beyond single-query or single-turn interactions. The proliferation of intelligent agents has opened up new modality for interacting with information, but these agents will need to be able to work more intelligently in understanding context and helping people at the task level. Several community events have taken place over the past few years focused on this topic (e.g., [27, 115, 148]) (PAIR Workshop, 2020; WICRS Workshop, 2020), indicating continual and increased interest by scholars, but also highlighting the need to do more in this important area. We believe there are three primary reasons for considering tasks while studying, designing, and evaluating IR systems.

1. As many scholars have argued for decades, IR systems should be helping people accomplish their tasks. The needs they express to such systems through queries or questions are just surface-level signals for the actual underlying problematic situation [31, 32]. Rather than assuming that everything we need to know about that situation is clearly expressed in those queries or questions, if we actually understand and model that situation or task, we may be able to develop better IR systems that go to the heart of people seeking information.

2. Often people are not able to express what they need or want. This is specifically the case for those with low information literacy, but it can also happen to regular users of IR systems and those with a good command on their search skills. For some time, librarians have addressed such situations with remarkable efficacy using reference interviews. For example, using Dervin's sense-making questions [85], one can probe an information seeker with appropriate questions that go beyond what they are explicitly asking. This process leads to an enhanced understanding of the underlying need and what support the person could use. Most existing IR systems lack this functionality. Trying to understand one's task could bring that valuable process of reference interviewing back into search.

3. There are emerging modalities and interaction styles that warrant an understanding of user's task. These include devices and methods that support natural, often voice-based, interactions. The systems, specifically intelligent agents, that power such interactions could benefit immensely from task-based knowledge. Such knowledge could help them engage with the user in a conversation, elicit information that may not be explicitly expressed, and be proactive in making recommendations in appropriate ways given the context.

In short, task knowledge can help us not only make existing IR systems more useful, but also allow us to create transformative solutions with emerging modalities that intelligent agents can support. To better understand these two cases, we will examine two different scenarios.

1.3   SEARCH ENGINE SCENARIO

Let us consider the following set of queries issued to a search engine by the same user during a single search session.

1. nigerian scam email

2. nigerian scam unemployment

3. washington unemployment scam

4. email for reporting unemployment scam

5. contact for reporting unemployment scam

How do we understand these queries? We can certainly examine each of these independently and provide an interpretation. A search engine, in a simplest sense, does just that. For example, when it looks at the second query, it will provide relevant documents about several Nigerian scams, with the one relating to unemployment filing toward the top. But then for the fourth query, it will provide documents that may contain email for filing for unemployment benefits. However, this is missing an important link. If we were to analyze the flow of the queries, it is clear that the searcher here is possibly a victim of Nigerian scam that targeted Washington state unemployment benefits during the COVID-19 pandemic in the U.S.[1] This person is now looking for a way to report this or contact someone for advice on how to proceed. That is their task, their intent. However, in terms of queries, this is divided up in two or three parts and when a search engine treats these parts separately instead of considering them as a part of a task, it leads to results and assistance that do not address the task directly.

Of course, you could argue that the search engines are not meant to simply hand over answers to complex tasks and that people need to connect the dots. That may be true for many

---

[1]https://www.seattletimes.com/business/economy/washington-adds-more-than-145000-weekly-jobless-claims-as-coronavirus-crisis-lingers/

Table 1.1: Envisioning a search engine that derives task information from queries and clicks

Queries and Clicks	Task Interpretation
Nigerian scam email [No click]	Find information about Nigerian scam email
Nigerian scam unemployment [Click on a WIRED story]	Find stories related to Nigerian scam email and/or unemployment
Washington unemployment scam [Click on a Seattle Times story]	Find stories related to Nigerian scam email and/or unemployment concerning Washington state
Email for reporting unemployment scam [Clicks on Department of Labor and FTC sites]	Find email for knowing/reporting Nigerian scam and/or unemployment concerning Washington state
Contact for reporting unemployment scam [No clicks]	

of the tasks and for many of the people, but not all the tasks all the time. This is specifically concerning to those with low information literacy such as seniors.

Now, let us ask what could be an alternative scenario. Imagine we have a search engine that not only considers these queries and the associated result clicks (all search engines do), but also connects the dots like we did before to try to understand the task. What would it look like? We envision that in Table 1.1.

What can be seen in the above table is actually not that far-fetched.

Existing search systems already consider clicks and other signals associated with a query. What is proposed here is going a few steps further to estimate *why* someone may be performing those queries and clicks. There are limitations, of course. We will probably never be able to tell what was going on in searchers' minds when they were running these queries, nor the real reason behind this search session. Were they really looking for something like this because they want to act on it or simply to fulfil their curiosity? Was this their own need or were they doing this for someone else? Will they take what they found here to fulfil a different or a bigger task or is this the start and end of the actual task for them? Despite accepting our limitations regarding how much we could learn from what we could observe here (e.g., queries, clicks, amount of time spent on them), there is quite a bit we could interpolate and extrapolate here that can bring us closer to knowing and addressing the underlying task, as demonstrated in Table 1.1.

1.4   INTELLIGENT AGENT SCENARIO

Now we will envision a scenario with a futuristic intelligent agent. You can imagine the following conversation happening with that agent over voice modality using a smart speaker, a smartphone, or some other device that is yet to be invented.

> **User**: I think I would like to go do some outside activity today. Do I need to wear a face mask if I go running?
>
> **Agent**: It depends where you are running, but if you are concerned about safety and still want an outdoor activity, may I suggest biking?
>
> **User**: Oh.. ya, sure, that could work. Do I need to know anything?
>
> **Agent**: While you don't need to wear a mask while biking, you should still bring one with you. There is also a chance of some rain showers, so plan for that. And yes, definitely carry some water.

Now let us see what may be going on here. There are four distinct features that we see the agent exhibiting.

- *Understanding the intention behind a user seeking information.* The agent understands that the user wants to do outdoor activity while being safe.[2] This understanding leads to the agent being able to make other recommendations than simply answering the asked question.

- *Addressing "people don't know what they don't know."* The user asked "what do I need to know if I go biking?", indicating their lack of knowledge about even what may be the right questions to ask. This often happens in human–human interactions. However, our current systems are not good at handling such questions. Here, the agent understands the situation (task), as well as the intention behind that question and responds with relevant suggestions.

- *Zero-query recommendations.* The user does not ask about weather, but the agent deems it important to convey that information as it may affect the outdoor activity. Also, given the nature of the activity (biking), the agent also recommends carrying water. These are examples are *zero-query recommendations*, in which an answer is provided without there being a clear question. Again, doing something like this requires a deep understanding of the situation (task), the user, and their intentions.

- *Proactive recommendations.* The conversation starts by the user asking a question about running, but rather than completely answering that question, the agent makes a different suggestion (biking), which turns out to be a better one. This is a case of the agent being proactive. In order to go beyond the user's need (at least the expressed need) and

---

[2]Note that this example of was created at the time of the COVID-19 pandemic, when face masks were required for many public activities to reduce the spread of the virus.

provide a relevant and compelling answers or recommendations, an agent needs to be able to understand the purpose behind the potential task, the user's intention behind asking a question, and the world knowledge about how different tasks are executed.

In short, in order to create an intelligent agent like the one envisioned in the scenario above, we need to bring in the following capabilities.

- Abstracting out from a query or a question or even an observation to the task and/or context.

- Leveraging world knowledge about public health guidelines and mask mandates.

- Generating recommendations based on that task/context and weighing if that would be better than query/question-based recommendation.

- Learning how to do a task.

As you can see, much (not all) of what we need to do revolves around tasks. This is just a simple example of a short conversation. Imagine having discussions (and even debates) about health, politics, and more. Imagine carrying out such conversations across multiple sessions, multiple devices, and even involve multiple people. There are tremendous possibilities here for a giant leap for IR systems. We believe at its core is the notion of task and ways to capture, represent, and address it. This book is intended to get you started on that journey. Before we go forward, let us see where we are. There has been considerable attention given to task-based search and recommendation in the recent years, which we will discuss in the next chapter. There have also been several community events in this space, indicating the growing interest and scholarly outcomes.

1.5   RECENT EVENTS AROUND TASK-BASED IR

Several workshops have been held in the space of task-based IR. Many of these workshops have focused on search interactions, searcher intents and tasks in information search, including ACM SIGCHI 2012 workshop on *End-user Interactions with Intelligent Systems* [297] organized by Simone Stumpf, Margaret Burnett, Volkmar Pipek, and Weng-Keen Wong, and the *Second Strategic Workshop on Information Retrieval in Lorne (SWIRL)* [8]. In 2012, Birger Larsen, Christina Lioma, and Arjen de Vries organized the *Task-based and Aggregated Search Workshop* [173], which focused on the challenges of task-based and aggregated search, such as the mismatch between search interface and specialized task-based functionalities, the lack of homogeneous systems to support different tasks, and so on. One of the significant contributions of this early workshop was that it identified how and to what extent domain-specific search and recommendation systems could be developed to support task level activities. Participants also discussed how a search system should be modified in order to provide better support for task-based search. In the same year, Nicholas Belkin, Charles Clarke, Ning Gao, Jaap Kamps, and

Jussi Karlgren organized the ACM SIGIR 2012 workshop entitled *"Entertain Me" Supporting Complex Search Tasks* [33]. The interactive workshop brought together researchers from different backgrounds focused on fostering potential solutions to problems faced by searchers with complex information needs. Aiming to support searchers during their entire search sessions when interactively solving a complex task, the workshop explored many aspects of interactive information systems such as complex search episodes, queries, exploratory search, understanding of search context, and finally, how to incorporate task and searcher context into an information system.

In an ACM SIGIR 2013 workshop on *Modeling User Behavior for Information Retrieval Evaluation* [70], participants examined ways to model search intent based on queries. They also identified problems with the use of queries as a proxy for search intent and brainstormed better solutions. In the first and second workshops on *Supporting Complex Search Tasks* organized by Maria Gade, Mark Hall, Hugo Huurdeman, Jaap Kamps, Marijn Koolen, Mette Skov, Elaine Toms, David Walsh [102], and Nicholas Belkin, Toine Bogers, Jaap Kamps, Diane Kelly, Marjin Koolen, and Emine Yilmaz [27], respectively, in 2015 and 2017 also prepared to initiate an interdisciplinary dialogues among researchers from information retrieval, information behavior, human–computer interaction (HCI), and computer science addressing many task-related open research questions. Participants tackled issues related to six aspects of information seeking—context, tasks, heterogeneous sources and search process, user interfaces (UI) and user experience (UX), and evaluation of systems. The workshops were helpful in fostering new collaborations among different communities to address these issues.

A more recent workshop hosted at ACM WSDM 2018 entitled *Learning from User Interactions* [213] and organized by Rishabh Mehrotra, Ahmed Awadallah, and Emine Yilmaz, focused on task-based intelligent systems, more specifically at six related topics: user needs and tasks understanding; user modeling and personalization; metrics and evaluation; user interaction processes and context; intelligent interface design; and applications. The workshop attracted participants from IR, human factors, ubiquitous computing, data mining, and other related domains. The ACM WSDM 2019 *Task Intelligence Workshop* [115], organized by Ahmed Awadallah, Mark Sanderson, Cathal Gurrin, and Ryen White, focused on various topic related to tasks in the context of system development including areas such search assistance, personalization, and recommendation.

Finally, we delivered a tutorial on this topic at SIGIR 2020 conference [279]. It was well-attended despite (or due to) the conference being virtual.

1.6 SUMMARY

In this chapter, we saw how task is or can be a core notion in an intelligent search or recommendation system. The idea that task is important to understand is not new, but most IR systems were built on the assumption that if we cater to individual requests well, we would be helping the information seekers accomplish their tasks too. Here we saw that not only that assumption can be flawed, but we may also be missing some wonderful opportunities to build truly intelligent search and recommendation systems. We saw this through a couple of scenarios with search system and a futuristic intelligent agent. In all, we hope you are convinced at this point that for a number of reasons, task-based IR is worth pursuing. The rest of the book is meant to provide a foundation for just that. The following are the specific objectives to be addressed in this book.

- Recognize **situations** where task knowledge can be useful in fulfilling a person's need and in helping them complete their current task.

- Discuss various **methods** to extract task information (both from log data and in real-time), including the topic (what), people's strategies and processes (how), and their intentions (why).

- Describe various types of **task support** offered by search engines, digital assistants, and task management applications.

- Outline different evaluation **metrics** for assessing the performance of task-based search and recommendation systems.

- Identify **challenges and opportunities** in making progress in this area and the role that the IR community can play.

We will begin in the next chapter by asking how IR scholars have studied task so far—specifically, extracting task information and representing that information.

CHAPTER 2

Task Frameworks, Expressions, and Representations

Before we take a deep dive into how task information is extracted and used in IR, it is important to review some background. This chapter covers how the notion of how task fits into a broader view of IR (search and recommender systems, specifically), along with how it has been positioned and studied over the years in the literature. The chapter also provides pointers to some of the relevant events in the recent past in this space.

2.1   HOW IS TASK STUDIED IN IR?

Rooted in the cognitive perspective, the task-based approach in information seeking and retrieval emerged within the interactive IR (IIR) community with studies conducted by Vakkari [311] and Ingwersen and Järvelin [126], which consider tasks in the design of IR systems to find out for what purposes the system is used [259] and thus provides implications for IR system design to personalize information according to the task at hand. Based on a series of empirical works, Vakkari [311] developed a general framework of task-based information searching which consists of three stages: *pre-focus*, *focus formulation*, and *post-focus*.

Many early works investigated and identified various aspects of task and especially the interactive nature of search tasks. Bates' [23] berrypicking model showed the interactive process of searching. The aim of task-based studies is to investigate the relationships between task characteristics and information seeking behaviors by recognizing and understanding the nature of different tasks and goals and designing IR systems which can support the accomplishment of a variety of such tasks and goals. Here, the task is a multi-level information seeking process in which people need information to achieve a goal to fulfill the task (e.g., [54, 259, 268, 310]). Many existing task models (e.g., [58, 149, 183]) have investigated and identified searchers' tasks as static and overarching goals that motivate search actions, but as we will see later, this is not always desired as the task evolves with time and changing cognitive states in the searcher.

Conversely, different characteristics or facets of tasks [183] influence people's interaction with intelligent systems, for example, when a searcher searches for information using a search engine [194]. Search tasks are influenced by the work task or everyday life task that drives them to seek information or are associated with a problematic situation [53]. Also, accomplishing more complex tasks requires more complex actions that are manifested throughout the session because complex tasks take longer to complete or require more queries [14, 112].

Apart from task, existing studies in IR segment information seeking behaviors into various levels of explicit and implicit signals. While performing tasks, searchers' actions are also driven by intentions and can be well-defined or ill-defined [126]. These studies have indicated that there is a close association between searchers' performance of a task and the information need, the search strategies employed, and the assessment of document relevance and utility.

Thus, an understanding of searchers' information seeking goals at the task level is essential to improve intelligent systems because different searchers have different needs and intentions; they face different problems in different situations. The usefulness or relevance of the information for a searcher may vary based on that searcher's specific situation or the context in which the information is needed or used. As the information searching session progresses, a searcher interacts with new information, which may change their state of knowledge, thus changing their needs and usefulness of documents. As a result, without considering the evolving nature of dynamic tasks, the recommendations provided by a search system may not be useful to a searcher in their current situation.

Recent industrial recommendation systems have relied heavily on large-scale user logs to obtain contextual information and build recommendation models. Recommendation models fall into one of the three categories—collaborative filtering, content-based filtering, and a hybrid of them. Collaborative filtering is a type of exploratory method which makes automatic filtering of information based on clusters of user characteristics and interests [270]. The underlying assumption of the collaborative filtering approach is that if a certain number of users have similar interests, then another user is more likely to have their opinion for a given item. The content-based filtering is an exploitative approach which uses only attributes of the items a user has previously consumed to model that user's preferences [315]. This algorithm tries to recommend items that are similar to those that a user liked in the past. However, each of these two methods has some limitations, for example, collaborative filtering performs poorly for cold-start problems, and a content-based approach is prone to sparsity problems. There is another approach that has recently been famous and more accurate—a hybrid method, which is essentially a combination of both collaborative and content-based filtering approach [22].

In recent years, advanced machine learning and deep learning model-based recommendations have made enormous progress and somewhat succeeded in solving recommendation problems [69]. By extracting meaningful latent factors from highly diverse and complex heterogeneous data, deep learning models such as matrix factorization, auto-encoders, memory networks, neural networks with collaborative filtering can achieve better recommendations [116, 184]. Furthermore, incorporating structure-based or feature-based knowledge graphs with a sequential learning or alternative learning approaches into a recommendation system have been shown to improve its performance [325]. Reinforcement learning-based approaches leverage feedback generated from people's continuously evolving interactions with the system, along with historical data, to generate recommendations [374].

However, various attributes of people and their interests used by sophisticated learning methods cannot fully capture contextual information about searchers, their search situation, the nature of the search task, etc., thus limiting the efficiency of recommendations based on these features. An effective intelligent system should incorporate searchers' short-term and long-term search goals, along with continually shifting user feedback data over a whole search session, while providing relevant information. Despite some progress in this area, there are still a lack of workable methods to connect predefined, static task properties and the dynamic transitions of task states.

Beyond search, tasks permeate almost every aspect of our daily work and personal lives [9]. They involve different activities, have different constraints, and take different amounts of time to complete. Some tasks can be completed quickly, while others take much longer, sometimes spanning several days or weeks. Task management applications such as Microsoft To Do, Google Tasks, and Todoist help people track their pending and completed tasks. Studies have found that users of these and similar systems would benefit from assistance with many aspects of task management, especially task planning [35]. Scheduling and prioritizing tasks are both challenging [235]. There has been some recent progress in task intelligence, in areas such as discovering digital assistant capabilities [334], estimating how long tasks will take to complete [341], and automatically tracking task status over time [342].

2.2   EXPLICIT EXPRESSION OF TASKS

While most of the prior research we find in the IR literature and most of how we would cover task in this book are around the idea of task being implicitly contained in user actions or intentions, there are times when the user explicitly expresses their task. This can be seen typically in task management applications, such as those mentioned above. Before we look at implicitly expressed tasks and ask questions about how to extract and represent those tasks, let us look at a more direct representation of user tasks—in to-do lists. Later in this book (Section 4.1), we will see how such tasks can be connected to search.

Tasks in to-do lists can be divided into two broad categories: actionable and non-actionable. An actionable task is something that one can readily act on. Examples include "buy a backpack," "find a new doctor," and "milk" in a grocery list. Non-actionable tasks are typically lists of things that serve as reminders or a way of notetaking. Examples include a list of books to read, and things to bring on a camping trip. They also include intangible, vague, or overly broad things, such as "make a difference."

Studies of to-do tasks have focused on task management, including how people plan and organize their tasks [35]. The recent availability of large-scale logs has enabled methods such as task duration estimation [341, 347], task completion detection [342], and enhancing notifications to maximize completion [104]. Systems have supported task completion by allowing users to focus on tasks requiring human intervention [20, 235] or by generating action plans [163]. Stumpf et al. [296] and Kiseleva et al. [158] explore methods to understand people's task intent and provide the resources required to complete those tasks, albeit not focused on to-do tasks and the connection between such tasks and search.

2.3   IMPLICIT EXPRESSION OF TASKS

A substantial portion of IR literature that deals with task is devoted to tasks being implicitly present in user actions, behaviors, or intentions. This notion creates challenges and opportunities. How do we explicate those tasks? How do we represent them? Are there specific number of tasks? Do tasks need to be well-defined or can they be "fuzzy"? If we have a representation for a task, how do we use it in an IR application? In the coming chapters, we will address these questions through a series of case studies. But for now, let us seek to better understand how implicit expression of tasks is studied in IR. We will divide up our discussion in various sections that group these studies into different ways to think about a task.

2.3.1   TASK LEVELS

According to Byström and Hansen [52, 53], task contexts in information practices can be represented by a nested model consisting of three levels (from outer level to inner level): work task, information seeking task, and search task (see Figure 2.1). Specifically, work tasks are separable parts of a person's duties in his or her workplace [53]. Note that not every sub-task within a work task can be transformed into an information seeking task. In many cases, some parts of a work task need system and human supports that are beyond the capacity of search systems (e.g., writing a dissertation proposal). In addition to the tasks generated in workplaces, everyday life tasks that emerge from non-work scenarios can also lead to active information seeking and searching practices (e.g., search for and book a hotel for travel) [4].

Information seeking tasks are a central component of information-intensive work tasks and may be deconstructed into general stages, including task construction, task performance, and task completion [52]. To identify the implicit information seeking task(s) within a work task, people need to analyze the information that is needed as well as the availability of various information resources and supports. This analysis is influenced by both work task properties and the task performer's knowledge and experience of using information resources.

Information search tasks focus on the satisfaction of a separable fraction of an information need through a single consultation of a source or sources (especially search systems) [53]. Many facets of a search task are significantly affected by the corresponding properties of the overarching work task [181]. Due to the integration of search support and general artificial intelligence, many recently developed intelligent systems (e.g., Google Assistant, Amazon Alexa) seek to go beyond simple search tasks and to directly support actions of different types in information-intensive work tasks (e.g., estimate task duration and arrange schedules [341], provide conversational guided task support [319]).

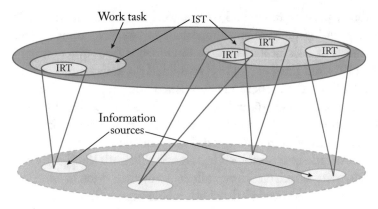

Legend: IST stands for information seeking task;
IRT stands for information search task

Figure 2.1: Byström and Hansen's model of task levels [52].

In addition to Byström and Hansen's nested model of task [52], Xie [356] also explored the multilevel nature of user goals and tasks and developed a four-level hierarchical framework of goals, including long-term goals (e.g., users' personal interests), leading search goals or work tasks, current search goals (current information seeking and search tasks), and interactive intentions (things that a user wants to accomplish in local steps or stages of search). This four-level typology covers a wide range of user goals and tasks (from long-term task-independent goals to local goals behind specific search tactics) and was verified by a series of user studies [186, 356].

To fully understand the role of tasks, it is also important to explore the value and impact of information seeking and searching that go beyond specific task contexts. Although many information seeking episodes are driven and shaped by tasks of different levels, it does not mean that the influence of information seeking and searching is restricted within the immediate task contexts. Instead, many information seeking and search tasks actually serve as the opportunities for users to enhance the metacognitive, information-literate skills that are often required for long-term learning and critical thinking [287] and to adjust their respective cognitive spaces and images of the external world [125]. Therefore, when conceptualizing and examining tasks in human-information interaction, researchers need to consider both task-centric factors and learning-centric elements. The investigation of different levels of tasks (including the long-term, learning-oriented aspect that goes beyond immediate task scenarios) can generate distinct focuses and metrics for search system evaluations.

2.3.2 TASK FACETS

To gain a comprehensive understanding of the impacts of tasks on information seeking and search behaviors at multiple levels, information seeking and IIR researchers have explored a variety of task dimensions or facets and sought to classify tasks on the basis of one or multiple dimensions. Focusing on different dimensions or task taxonomies, previous research has examined the impacts of task facets on search interactions from different perspectives. For instance, Liu et al. [191] and Jiang et al. [134] examined the associations between user behaviors and objective task features (i.e., task product, task goal, task type) and discussed to what extent these behavioral features can help disambiguate search tasks of different types. Capra et al. [58] found that manipulating task *a priori* determinability via modifying task items and dimensions can significantly affect users' perceived task difficulty and choices of search strategies.

With respect to task-user combined features, Wildemuth [348] argued that in task-based information search, users' search tactics are influenced by their domain knowledge related to task topics. Liu et al. [192] demonstrated that both whole-session level and within-session search behaviors are affected by task difficulty, and that the dynamic relationships between search behavior and task perception are subject to the influence of task type (i.e., single fact-finding, multiple fact-finding, and multiple-piece information gathering). Similarly, Aula, Khan, and Guan [13] also investigated search behavioral variations under tasks of different levels of difficulty. By conducting a lab study and a large-scale online study, they found that when performing difficult search tasks, users tend to issue more diverse queries (have a more unsystematic query refinement process), use advanced operators more frequently, and spend longer time on search engine result pages (SERPs) during their search processes.

Given that many IIR studies only examine one or a few task dimensions, Li and Belkin [183] developed a faceted approach to conceptualizing tasks in IR based on related literature on task classification as well as their empirical studies on task-based information searching [181, 182]. The faceted framework provides a holistic approach to exploring the nature of tasks and conceptually supports a series of empirical studies on task-based search interactions. Several of the case studies later presented in this book will use this particular framework of task facets.

2.3.3 TASK STAGES

Task process is one of the facets of the task entity [183]. Differing from the static task properties (e.g., predefined task goal, task product), however, task process speaks to an alternative approach to understanding the nature of tasks. When conceptualizing tasks from the process-oriented perspective, we are essentially looking at the process of *doing tasks*. The core argument behind this perspective is that in the context of information seeking and searching, we cannot define or study a task without examining *how* the task was actually completed (or failed). Therefore, to fully understand a task, we need to explore both the objective task features and users' responses to the evolving task environments at multiple levels (e.g., behavioral, cognitive, emotional).

In the information seeking and IR communities, a series of classical models have been developed and applied to describe the general process of performing information seeking and search tasks. Many of these models mainly focus on the behavioral aspect of task process and

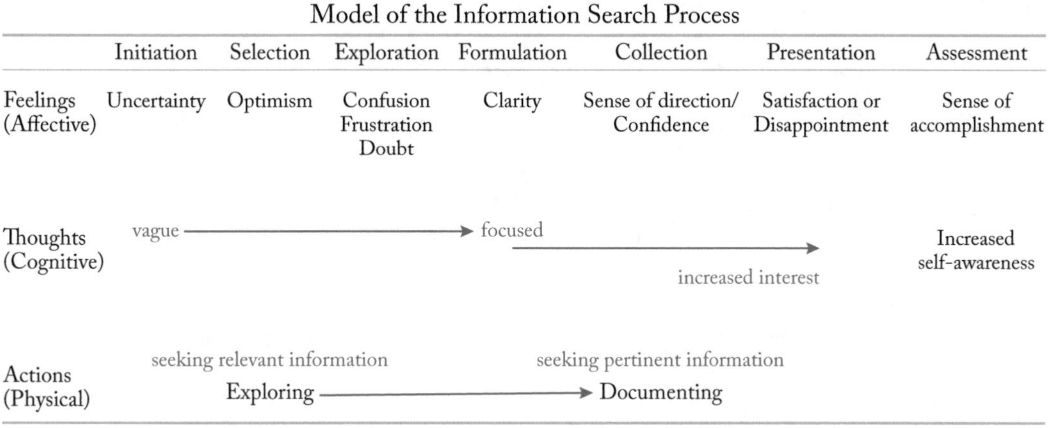

Model of the Information Search Process

	Initiation	Selection	Exploration	Formulation	Collection	Presentation	Assessment
Feelings (Affective)	Uncertainty	Optimism	Confusion Frustration Doubt	Clarity	Sense of direction/ Confidence	Satisfaction or Disappointment	Sense of accomplishment
Thoughts (Cognitive)	vague $\longrightarrow$			focused $\longrightarrow$ increased interest			Increased self-awareness
Actions (Physical)	seeking relevant information Exploring $\longrightarrow$			seeking pertinent information Documenting			

Figure 2.2: Kuhlthau's information search process (ISP) model [166].

look at the transitions of information seeking and search actions. For instance, to describe the general process of information seeking, Ellis [94] studied the information seeking patterns of academic social scientists and broke it down into six characteristics: starting, chaining, browsing, differentiating, monitoring, and extracting. Wilson [353] suggests that in some circumstances, Ellis' "characteristics" can be organized as a sequence of information seeking stages in a process model. Ellis' model clearly identifies the features of information seeking patterns and has been modified and tested based on empirical studies (e.g., [95, 96]). However, this model only describes the behavioral level of task-based information seeking. It does not consider the interaction between the information seeker and the multi-dimensional context in which task states and information seeking activities evolve.

Given the multidimensionality of information seeking activities, Kuhlthau's work complements that of Ellis by attaching to the stages of the "Information Search Process" (ISP) the associated affective states (e.g., uncertainty, sense of direction), cognitive states (e.g., vague, focused), and actions [166, 167] (see Figure 2.2). Similar to Ellis' framework, Kuhlthau's ISP model has also been tested in many empirical studies conducted in library and educational contexts (e.g., [26, 166, 168]). In addition, Kuhlthau [167] also proposes the principle of uncertainty that states that information commonly increases uncertainty in the early stages of the information seeking and search process. The increased uncertainty indicates a space for interactive systems to provide in-situ interventions and task-centric support. The concept of uncertainty in the ISP connects the affective level and the action level of information seeking and is also associated with certain cognitive states and problems in human-information interaction, such as anomalous state of knowledge in interactive information retrieval [28] and cognitive gap in the sense-making process [85]. Kuhlthau's ISP model is a useful tool for describing and qualitatively explaining the stages of information seeking at multiple levels. However, it offers limited

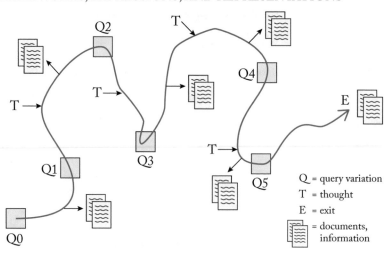

Figure 2.3: Bates's model of berrypicking, evolving search [23].

insights for understanding the variations in task states and behavioral changes within information search sessions. This is because the ISP model was developed in the context of long-term learning and information seeking tasks, and described the stages over month(s)-long periods rather than individual search sessions.

In the IR community, several models and techniques have been developed to describe and explain different aspects of tasks and search activities. Oddy [239] developed the THOMAS program for supporting users' dialogues with IR systems. This considers the shift in users' needs and emphases during search interactions and adjusts its information displays according to users' needs and reactions or judgments to the retrieved information. In contrast to the traditional relevance feedback model [263], which assumes that users' information needs are static (the only improving part is query formulation), the THOMAS model offers more room for users to express and shift their focuses during search iterations and the associated learning processes.

Another seminal model in the literature is the berrypicking model by Bates [23], proposed to describe the process of information searching. Bates argued that the classical single-query, best-match model cannot capture the interactive, evolving nature of information search tasks (see Figure 2.3). In the berrypicking model, the nature of queries is an evolving one, instead of single and static. Also, the search process follows a berrypicking, evolving process, rather than a linear sequence of steps leading to a single best retrieved set of relevant documents. In contrast to the traditional single-query model of ad hoc IR, the berrypicking model illustrates the interactive process of information searching and has been empirically supported by many task-based studies in the information seeking community [94, 166, 256, 295].

Spink [292] developed a multi-level model of search and identifies user judgments, search tactics, interactive feedback loops, and cycles as constituting the search process of an IR system

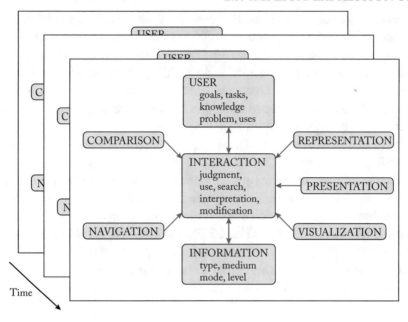

Figure 2.4: Koenemann and Belkin's model of user-centered search interaction [161].

user in tasks of different types. Based on Kuhlthau's ISP model as well as a series of empirical studies, Vakkari [311] proposed a general framework of task-based information searching, which consists of three task stages: pre-focus, focus formulation, and post-focus. His studies also indicate that there is a close association between the participants' problem states in task performance and the information need, the search tactics employed and the assessment of document relevance and utility. Belkin [30] proposed a conceptual model that represents session-level information seeking episodes as a sequence of users' iterative interactions with an interactive search system and the retrieved information objects (e.g., search result snippets, documents) (illustrated in Figure 2.4). The focus of Belkin [30]'s search session model is a user-centered search interaction that varies over time under the influence of task(s), goal(s), and an evolving problematic situation. Although Belkin [30] did not specify the states and state transition patterns in a search session, he clearly emphasized the basic ideas of modeling temporal changes in search interactions and developing dynamic support for users according to search task properties.

The classical models discussed above are widely applied in describing the process and stages of tasks, information seeking, and searching. However, most, if not all of them, offers limited implications for building computational frameworks of task processes and designing practical, dynamic supports for complex tasks at different moments.

To address this issue, some researchers have developed computationally congenial models for representing task states or stages, simulating task-based search interactions, and evaluating recommendations of different types. For instance, Cole et al. [74] investigated user activity patterns in tasks of different types and demonstrated that task types and levels of task difficulty can be represented and disambiguated by the sequence and distributions of user activity states (derived from page visiting behaviors) and cognitive processing states (approximated using eye movement patterns). Similarly, Dung and Fuhr [90] adopted both discrete and continuous search behavioral signals and developed a Hidden Markov Model (HMM) for recognizing the search phases and analyzing the transitions among them.

To develop an effective formal model of search interactions, Fuhr [101] proposed a framework for extending probabilistic IR to the IIR context and representing users' situation transitions and choices at different moments of information searching episodes. He found that within the proposed cost model of interaction, the expected benefit of a single choice can be maximized, which forms the basis for the derivation of the optimum ordering of choices (i.e., the probability ranking principle for interactive IR, or IIR-PRP). The IIR-PRP model serves as an important step toward building a computational framework for supporting the functional design of interactive search systems. However, this model abstracts out a variety of user characteristics and lacks effective representations of the task states and associated cognitive variations.

2.4   COMPLEX SEARCH TASKS

As it is discussed in the previous sections, an important area of IIR research involves understanding and measuring the impacts of task facets on search behaviors, experiences, and performances. *Task complexity* is one facet that has received considerable attention. Understandably, most of the works in the literature that we find around tasks either assume or explicitly suggest dealing with complex tasks. Going through a process of explicating, representing, and applying task information may not be advantageous for simple tasks. Besides, most existing IR systems are already quite effective at dealing with simple requests or tasks.

Based on different task properties, researchers have developed multiple frameworks to define task complexity in the context of information seeking and searching. For instance, Byström and Järvelin [54] studied the impacts of work task complexity on information seeking and use and developed a five-class complexity framework. Based on a qualitative investigation, they found that in complex tasks, the intentions of understanding, sense-making and problem formulation are essential and require different types of information through a variety of information sources at different points of information seeking episodes.

Kelly et al. [149] explored the cognitive complexity of tasks and adopted Bloom's taxonomy of learning domains [42] in characterizing different levels of search task complexity. Their results indicate that complex search tasks (e,g., analyze, evaluate, create) required significantly more search activities from users (e.g., more issued queries, clicks, and dwell time on visited pages and documents). Ghosh, Rath, and Shah [103] employed Kelly's framework of task complexity in their user study on searching in learning-oriented tasks. They found that tasks of different cognitive complexities varied significantly in information search patterns (the transitions of search tactics) and learning performances.

Capra et al. [58, 59] used tasks *a priori* determinability (i.e., the level of uncertainty about task outcomes and processes) as a representation of task complexity and argued that the variations in needed items and the clarity of dimensions for result evaluation can significantly affect the overall task determinability.

Liu et al. [194] extracted two major static task facets: *task product* and *task goal*, from Li and Belkin's faceted framework [183] and used the combination of these two facets to represent and measure task complexity. They found that tasks of different levels of complexity (e.g., factual-product, specific-goal tasks, intellectual-product, amorphous-goal tasks) can be represented by different patterns of local information seeking intentions in search iterations and search actions. Sarkar et al. [267] also represented task complexity using the unique combinations of task product and task goal and investigated the patterns of the search problems that users encountered during task process. They found that in tasks of varying levels of complexity, users encountered different search obstacles, preferred different support from systems, and adopted distinct search strategies. Moreover, this difference in task complexity, encountered problems, and preferred system help can to some extents be inferred from users' search behaviors.

The last few years have seen the information seeking and IR communities tackle more complex search tasks that involve multiple rounds of distinct search actions and active transitions of cognitive states [83, 164]. Many of the existing studies represented different levels of task complexity using one (e.g., task determinability, complexity of learning goals) or more (e.g., combinations of task facet values) static task features and revealed some of the behavioral effects of complex search tasks. However, there has been little data-driven work representing complex tasks as sequences of cognitive and behavioral states in forms suitable for computational modeling. As a result, we still lack an effective approach to exploring the connections between predefined, static task properties and the distribution and dynamic transitions of multidimensional task states. This analytical approach is critical, especially for developing adaptive search systems that can go beyond simple, static task properties and support users according to their current task states (i.e., reactive support [124]) or even the prediction of their subsequent states (i.e., proactive support [196]).

2.5   REPRESENTING TASKS

Efforts in understanding user needs and tasks are not new [29]; however, task information extraction and representation have remained a challenging problem as tasks can be defined at different granularity levels and vary by users. Past studies have classified tasks into many types based on various task features, for example, closed tasks and open-ended tasks [209], specific and general tasks [245], factual, descriptive, instrumental, and exploratory tasks [156], fact-finding and information gathering tasks [305], and tasks to learn about a topic, make a decision, find out how to, find facts, and find a solution [99]. Li and Belkin [183] provided a comprehensive classification scheme, which includes several dimensions such as task product, objective complexity, subjective complexity, and difficulty.

Another large body of research has focused on the problem of segmenting and organizing large user search logs into semantically coherent structures to identify users' tasks and search contexts. Many of these studies have defined an in-session search task as an atomic information need resulting in one or more queries [137]. Most previous work has focused on users' search behavior analysis and prediction within a single search session, where a session refers to a sequence of search activities ended by a prolonged period of inactivity [336]. Many studies have extracted in-session tasks [137, 202] while others have identified cross-session tasks [165, 323] from query sequences in search logs based on various classification and clustering methods. The cross-session task consists of a sequence of queries that resembles a distinct, high-level information need. Also, most prior research has focused on segmenting chronologically ordered search queries into higher-level search tasks. Many recent works have also investigated multi-session information needs, called search tasks [14, 165, 180, 312, 323].

In contrast, previous research has relied on the varied definition of tasks [183, 312]. In most cases, search tasks consist of many different yet related needs or goals that require different sets of queries to fulfill those different multi-aspect information needs. Such tasks are defined as complex search tasks [14, 137]. Complex tasks often tend to have multiple sub-tasks associated with them, and search logs can be visualized as complicated compositions of tasks and sub-tasks, with complex search tasks decomposed into more focused sub-tasks. More recently, Mehotra et al. [215, 218] proposed two Bayesian nonparametric methods to extract sub-tasks from a complex task and recursively extract hierarchies of tasks and sub-tasks.

Session identification within a search process is a common strategy used to develop macro-level task representations [14, 120, 137, 202, 203, 323]. Sessions provide a look beyond individual queries, preserve semantic associations between query trails, and maintain user activity context. Strategies for session identification from log data have been extensively studied. Initially, studies have used content-based features [282] such as the lexical content of queries for determining the topical change in the sequence of query formulations. Temporal features [77] have also used to segment sessions, such as identifying the inactivity threshold between logged activities and used that time to separate sessions. Later, [247] combined two methods and used a 30-minute timeout together with query similarity measures to define sequences of similar queries that combine to form query chains within a session. In two different studies, Cao and colleagues [56, 57] analyzed and represented search context similar to task representations by modeling sessions as sequences of user queries and clicks.

A majority of recent task representation works have explored query contents and other query-related features to model tasks from search logs. Jones et al. [137] tried to extract tasks based on query terms, query reformulations, click entropy, URL domain clicked, query length, post-click actions, and session lengths. Radlinski et al. [248] investigated tasks based on query reformulations and clicks using random walk on the bipartite query-document click graph. Lucchese et al. [201–203] exploited session-based queries and the knowledge collected by Wiktionary and Wikipedia for detecting query pairs based on semantics and propose several clustering algorithms and a novel efficient heuristic algorithm for extracting tasks from a given query collection. They clustered queries by dropping query-pairs with low weights. In another study, Lucchese et al. [200] explored the concept of related tasks using a "task relation graph" as a representation of users' search behaviors on a task-by-task perspective. Wang et al. [323] adopted a structured learning approach in partitioning tasks by separating query sequences based on latent features (e.g., query-based features: query term cosine similarity; URL-based features: Jaccard coefficient between clicked URL sets; session-based features: same session and the number of sessions in between). They tried to identify search tasks based on clustering queries into tasks by finding the most vital link between a candidate query and queries in the target cluster.

Conversely, Blei et al. [41] took a topical similarity approach to cluster queries based on similarities between query topics to identify tasks. Their model assumed that two queries belong to the same search task if they issued in a fixed or flexible time period and used Latent Dirichlet Analysis (LDA) to cluster queries into topics based on the query co-occurrences within the same time-frame. Li et al. [179] also modeled temporal query patterns using Hawkes processes and combine the topic model with Hawkes processes to identify and label search tasks. They assumed that queries that are temporally proximal belong to the same task, and different users with the same information needs tend to submit topically coherent queries. Verma and Yilmaz [317] tried to identify entities and cluster of terms related to entities in queries (e.g., using tagging, TF-IDF scoring, term filtering, category terms) to represent a task as a set of terms related to an entity. Assuming hierarchical structure of search process, Mehotra et al. [214–218] extracted tasks and related sub-tasks using Bayesian Rose Trees where each node of the tree represents a task, and each task represents a set of queries and task partition based on query-term similarity (cosine similarity between term sets of the queries, proportion of common terms between queries, Jaccard coefficient between terms of queries) URL-based similarity (the edit distance between URL pairs from the queries, Jaccard coefficient between URL sets from the queries), session/used based similarity (if the two queries belong to the same user and/or the same session), and embedding-based similarity (cosine distance between embedding vectors of the two queries). In another study, Mehotra and Yilmaz [219] employed a graph-based query-clustering approach based on finding weighted connected components of a graph. From a different perspective, Craswell and Szumner [80] identified tasks based on random walks on click graph between queries and documents. All of these efforts have led to promising, but often limited to certain domains or task types, results. Further development, testing, and reflections are needed to see how well we can recognize and integrate tasks in IR situations.

2.6   SUMMARY

As it should be evident from this chapter, task-related scholarship has had a long and profound history in IR and related fields. We saw how task is studied in various conceptualizations and frameworks for addressing information needs of a user. There have been several different frameworks for conceptualizing tasks. Often these frameworks allow us to understand a task after it has happened rather than as it happens. While this retrospective analysis is useful, it limits us from having meaningful information about a task in real-time to use in an IR application. Nonetheless, this perspective has been quite fruitful in the literature. Often, scholars use such frameworks to design tasks for their interactive IR studies.

It is important to note that when it comes to representing tasks, the frameworks or taxonomies that have finite facets or stages have clear advantages and disadvantages. Due to their specificity, they provide us clearly interpretable and explainable representations of tasks. They also make it easier to build models (e.g., classifiers), as we will see in Chapter 4. Conversely, such structured representations of tasks limit our ability to capture more variety of tasks in more contexts. There are also situations where a clear construct of task is not given or even needed; forcing an underlying situation to a predefined notion of task could hinder our ability to go beyond what the said construct or framework allows. Later in this book, specifically in Chapter 5, we will cover constructing task representations that are built with the available data and the knowledge of the situation rather than a specific framework with finite stages or facets.

CHAPTER 3

Using Task Construct in IR

As we saw in the previous chapter, many scholars have argued for decades that knowing about and using task information in an information interaction is essential for truly supporting the user and personalizing content and recommendations. Understanding and utilizing task knowledge goes beyond better personalization; it becomes an essential tool to help people discover information that they do not often know how to ask for—addressing the challenge of knowledge gaps or "people don't know what they don't know."

This chapter will show how, over the decades, the notion of *task* has been proposed, investigated, and used in various IR works. This includes multiple ways to think about *task*, integrate it in studying an IR situation, and finding ways to incorporate task knowledge to support various user activities. More importantly, through two case studies, we will see how the task construct can be used in studying IR situations. The first case study will describe efforts to understand how different task types contribute to source selection and search outcomes. It starts by showing how different task types are accounted for in an interactive IR study—not as a way to study task type effects, but as a way to be inclusive and offer more generalizable conclusions.

3.1 UNDERSTANDING EFFECTS OF TASK TYPES ON INFORMATION BEHAVIORS

As we observed previously, there is a growing realization among the scholars that the task type affects almost all other aspects of one's information seeking episode. Therefore, it is quite common for them to either carefully pick one kind of task or have multiple task types as independent variable. The former allows them to situate their findings with a specific task type, whereas the latter helps see how different kind of tasks affect information behaviors. We will take a couple of examples to see how such studies are conducted around task types.

3.1.1 CONNECTING TASK TYPE WITH INFORMATION SOURCES AND OUTCOMES

One of the hypotheses related to task types is that it should affect what kind of information sources users access and how they use the information retrieved from those sources. For instance, if a task is trivial in nature (e.g., finding movie show times), the searcher may not pay much attention to the trustworthiness of the source. Conversely, if the task involves making a consequential decision, e.g., about health-related matters, users will need or want to be more careful in where they find information, how deep they look into those sources, and how they decide to use that obtained information. In short, task types may affect people's information seeking behaviors as mediated by source selection.

We will start with a case study that uses different tasks, but more as a way to offer variety to searchers while collecting their behavioral data. In what follows, we will see how researchers constructed different tasks that are similar in nature, but have different topics.

This case study comes from Sarkar et al. [266]. The authors investigated the relationship between information seekers' selection and use of information sources and their perceptions of information seeking outcomes (i.e., successes and failures) in the context of information seeking barriers as well as contextual factors such as knowledge, emotion, and social role. For this, the authors recruited 53 participants, who performed four simulated information-seeking tasks over a two-day period and reported their experiences and findings in an online logbook. The authors also conducted semi-structured interviews with 23 participants to examine the issues that arose from the logbook.

Task topics were initially inspired by a qualitative survey on Mechanical Turk (MTurk) for another study that examined individuals' failures in information seeking (see Wang and Shah [330] for more details). The authors designed the tasks based on those that the study participants rated as highly difficult. While designing these tasks, the authors referred to Wilde-muth and Freund's [350] guideline that exploratory search tasks should provide specific context and situation while also offering flexibility in task outcomes, thus inspiring multi-stage and multi-faceted information seeking endeavors. Below are the task descriptions presented to the participants.

Task-1 (T1): Suppose you are preparing for a debate tournament. One of the topics will be whether abortion should be legal. Find at least five arguments that support legalizing abortion and five arguments that oppose legalizing abortion.

Task-2 (T2): Suppose you are considering purchasing a hybrid car and want to compare the pros and cons of different manufacturers and models (e.g., Honda, Ford, and Toyota). You also want your potential car to cost no more than $25,000. Please find a hybrid car model that fits your budget and requirement.

Task-3 (T3): Suppose you are writing a report to discuss whether cell phones are safe. Please find at least five arguments to support that cell phones are safe and five arguments to oppose it.

Task-4 (T4): Suppose you are looking for an affordable apartment (under $1000/month) in the city of Providence, Rhode Island that best matches your needs. You want the apartment to be in a convenient location (e.g., close to grocery stores, restaurants). You also want to consider the neighborhood (e.g., safety). Please find at least two apartments that satisfy your requirements.

The study produced 636 information seeking episodes related to the four tasks, 389 (61%) of which were successful, 93 (14.6%) of which were partially successful, and the remainder (154,

24.2%) were unsuccessful or failures. Participants decided to use impersonal sources (e.g., informational Websites) 457 (71.9%) times, and interpersonal sources (e.g., online forums, texting, online chat) 198 times (31.1%).

Going beyond using these tasks as a way to offer a variety of options to the searcher while collecting their data, the authors investigated how different tasks affected their source selection and the outcomes of their search processes [329]. Their findings can be summarized as follows.

- Impersonal sources positively affect the accuracy and relevance of information sources for all types of tasks, and adequacy and trustworthiness regardless of task type.

- Interpersonal sources negatively affect the adequacy, accuracy, and relevance of information sources for all types of tasks, and the trustworthiness of information sources for intellectual tasks as well as when task type is not considered.

- Websites (e.g., Kelley Blue Book) positively affect the accuracy, adequacy, and relevance of information sources for all types of tasks.

- Websites positively affect the trustworthiness of information sources for intellectual tasks as well as when all information seeking episodes were considered regardless of task type.

- Search engines positively affect the accuracy, adequacy, relevance, and trustworthiness of information sources for intellectual tasks as well as when all sessions were considered regardless of task type.

- Face-to-face communication negatively affects the accuracy of information sources for all task types as well as the adequacy and relevance for everyday life tasks, and regardless of task type.

- Online chatting or texting negatively affect the accuracy, adequacy, trustworthiness, and relevance of information sources regardless of task type.

- Online chatting or texting also negatively affect the accuracy, adequacy, and trustworthiness in intellectual tasks alone and the adequacy in everyday life tasks as well.

- Posting on online forums negatively affects the accuracy, adequacy, relevance, and trustworthiness of information sources regardless of task type.

Overall, participants largely used impersonal sources (231 times for everyday life tasks and 226 times for intellectual tasks). Among impersonal sources, they used professional websites (e.g., Kelley Blue Book) most frequently to find information. Regarding the influence of task type, the study could not find much difference in participants' ratings for impersonal sources across task type. Most participants rated all impersonal sources highly compared to interpersonal sources (ratings ranging from 3–5), irrespective of task type, and they scarcely gave them a low rating (ratings ranging from 1–2). On the contrary, there are some observable variations regarding participants' ratings for interpersonal sources. Notably, they rated interpersonal sources relatively higher in terms of accuracy, adequacy, relevance, and trustworthiness for everyday life tasks compared to intellectual tasks.

Statistical analysis revealed that interpersonal sources generally negatively affect all quality dimensions of information sources. In particular, chatting, texting, and posting online have negative effects on the ratings of all criteria when task type is not considered. It was also found that face-to-face communication negatively affects all but trustworthiness. Participants explained in their narratives that they usually relied on one or a few people's opinions or knowledge, which were inadequate given their limited personal experiences (e.g., P4: "They mostly had Toyota Priuses so it was difficult to have a great understanding of the hybrid market and what exactly is available.")

Although posting on online forums would have generated more information, it would also have taken longer so not enough information was collected on time (e.g., P50: "Not enough people responded to provide adequate results.") Also, interpersonal sources might not be as focused as expected and irrelevant topics could easily come up, which affected relevance of the information received (e.g., P51: "There wasn't much information included with the person's answer and opinion, and the answer quickly went off topic"). When considering each task type separately, texting and online chat's negative effects in intellectual tasks become more obvious, influencing the accuracy, adequacy, and trustworthiness of information. This is probably because chatting and texting may be more suitable for obtaining a quick answer. Intellectual tasks (in this specific study, preparing for debate topics) require more domain specific knowledge or scientific evidence that could not be easily obtained via these information sources, particularly from non-experts. Participants often believed that the information offered by others was merely non-expert opinion, so the accuracy and adequacy were doubtful (e.g., P30: "There is no scientific evidence to back any of this up;" P02: "Mainly this was one person's opinion on the topic, so it gets rated slightly lower").

Task type did influence participants' judgment of information quality along certain dimensions. For the everyday life tasks (T2 and T4), participants were more likely to seek a community of people with similar interests to help verify online information. Unlike intellectual tasks, in which participants perceived information accuracy from interpersonal sources to be low, everyday life tasks sometimes reflected participants' appreciation of other people's opinions (e.g., P30: "There's actually a large community for the type of vehicle. They would suggest maybe a list, check your local store, check this Website, check that Website;" P34: "I asked my group on Facebook. Their responses kind of verified that it was a decent area to live than the other areas").

Overall, this study clearly demonstrated that task type influenced participants' selections of information sources and quality judgment. For the everyday life decision-making tasks (T2 and T4), participants sought out people with similar interests to help verify the information found online. Meanwhile, they tended to distrust anyone who was associated with the business (e.g., salesperson, apartment manager): P13: "This interaction did nothing to get me my needed information. I cannot trust a salesperson to give totally relevant information because they're trying to sell a car." For the intellectual tasks, they highly rated websites with balanced and neutral arguments. The authors also concluded that task type affects users' evaluation of sources. For intellectual tasks, people seek balanced, neutral, or factual information from impersonal and interpersonal sources. Conversely, for everyday decision-making tasks, people want opinionated information from interpersonal sources and additional information from impersonal sources.

3.1.2 CONNECTING TASK TOPIC AND TASK TYPE

It is not uncommon to see *topic* and *task* being used interchangeably in the research literature or in discussions with human subjects. Other times, it is difficult to distinguish one from the other. Is "look for car insurance" a topic or a task? The purists will say that "car insurance" is the topic and looking for (or searching for, or shopping for) car insurance is the task. Does this distinction really matter? That is the question Hienert et al. [119] asked.

Topics are used to describe the scenario for a specific information need which may be described as a mixture of task type and topic. This is typically the case with TREC, organized by the U.S. National Institute of Standards and Technology (NIST).[1] TREC runs several tracks each year, most of which—such as the Core/Web Track [76]—provide topics for running experiments. Participating research teams often use these topic titles and/or descriptions as their tasks.

However, one should not always equate a topic with a task. As Kelly [146] points out, the topic describes the subject (area) of a task. This can be rather a broad domain (e.g., health or e-commerce used in [149]) or a very concrete theme or thing (e.g., a person). Kelly states that the topic represents the focus of the task and that the combination of a specific task and topic forms the information need [146]. On the user side, studies have examined how user knowledge may influence search behavior. Therefore, it can be distinguished between the broader idea of domain knowledge and the more specific idea of topic knowledge [369].

Hienert et al. [119] used data collected from four different tasks situated in the discipline of journalism, which try to capture different search problems in this area. Each of these tasks was conducted with two different topics: (1) "Coelacanth" and (2) "Methane Clathrates and Global Warming." Below are those tasks for the topic Coelacanth (a type of fish); the same schema was used for the second topic. Tasks were designed based on the task classification system proposed by [183] and modified in [74].

Task-1: Copy Editing (CPE)

Your assignment: You are a copy editor at a newspaper and you have only 20 minutes to check the accuracy of the six italicized statements in the excerpt of a piece of news story below.

---

[1]https://trec.nist.gov

Your task: Please find and save an authoritative page that either confirms or discon-firms each statement.

Task-2: Story Pitch (STP)

Your assignment: You are planning to pitch a science story to your editor and need to identify interesting facts about the coelacanth ("see-la-kanth"), a fish that dates from the time of dinosaurs and was thought to be extinct.

Your task: Find and save web pages that contain the six most interesting facts about coelacanths and/or research about coelacanths and their preservation.

Task-3: Relationships (REL)

Your assignment: You are writing an article about coelacanths and conservation ef-forts. You have found an interesting article about coelacanths but in order to develop your article you need to be able to explain the relationship between key facts you have learned.

Your task: In the following there are five italicized passages, find an authoritative web page that explains the relationship between two of the italicized facts.

Task-4: Interview Preparation (INT)

Your assignment: You are writing an article that profiles a scientist and their research work. You are preparing to interview Mark Erdmann, a marine biologist, about coelacanths and conservation programs.

Your task: Identify and save authoritative web pages for the following: Identify two (living) people who likely can provide some personal stories about Dr. Erdmann and his work. Find the three most interesting facts about Dr. Erdmann's research. Find an interesting potential impact of Dr. Erdmann's work.

Table 3.1 gives an overview of each task type with its task facets. Each participant searched for task types, each task on a different topic. The order of the 2 tasks and 2 topics was additionally flipped, yielding 16 different configurations.

The authors conducted a laboratory study with undergraduate students majoring in jour-nalism at Rutgers University and having completed at least one course in news writing. The 40 participants had to perform two search tasks (one on each topic), the annotation of bookmarks and search intents and had to complete several questionnaires.[2]

It was found that user behavior was not only dependent on the task type, but also on the task topic. The authors discovered a number of session variables that show significant differ-ences between the two topics in one task type, e.g., bookmark first session step or pages/search. Specifically, different dwell time measures show significant differences between topics. There

---

[2]The same study was used to collect other kinds of data too, mainly about search intentions, which we will discuss in the next section.

Table 3.1: Task types and their corresponding facets

Task Name	Task Facets			
	Product	Level	Goal	Named Items?
Copy editing	Find facts	Segment	Specific	Yes
Story pitch	Find facts	Segment	Amorphous	No
Article development	Produce ideas	Document	Amorphous	Yes
Interview preparation	Produce ideas	Document	Amorphous	No

are two reasons for this phenomenon: (a) In some cases (e.g., for Story Pitch with the task level 'Document segment') the authors found that high decision times originate from individual web pages containing a lot of text content. This meant that users needed more time to extract relevant information for the task. (b) In other cases, users spent more time on average on all content pages.

The authors also looked for overall correlations between subjective measures and session variables. This can be set in contrast to correlations found by dividing the dataset by task type or topic. For example, topic familiarity only showed a weak correlation for the topic Coelacanth, but not for Methane Clathrates and not for different task types. For correlations to task difficulty the session variables action count, task time and average first session step showed stable correlations for both topics, but not for each task type. Other correlations to post-difficulty are dependent on the topic. For the usefulness of bookmarks a number of correlation can be found for the topic Coelacanth (−0.610 to task time, −0.544 to bookmark total display time, and −0.493 to total time on content pages) which are weaker for Methane Clathrates.

From the analysis and the discussion the authors arrived at the following conclusions.

- Topic familiarity in this experiment overall only played a minor role because both topics were fairly unfamiliar to subjects. However, topic familiarity was dependent on the task topic.

- Task difficulty is moderately correlated to user effort and can be measured with a number of session variables such as task time, number of actions, or more specifically with features such as number of SERP visits or number of content pages. The correlation between user effort and task difficulty seems to be dependent on the task type and topic.

- Session variables measuring user behavior are also dependent on the task type and task topic.

- Task success and task difficulty are strongly negatively correlated, and task success can be measured with session variables such as task time and with session variables dependent on the topic.

- Task success and the usefulness of bookmarks interpreted as the task's result are nearly strongly related. This means the content's usefulness plays an important role for task success.

- Usefulness of bookmarks is weakly to moderately correlated to certain dwell times and dependent on the task type and topic.

- A threshold can be used to distinguish between useful (bookmarked) pages and other content pages. Decision time and total dwell time can be used as within-session variables independent of the task type and topic.

- Decision time on web pages can be dependent on the text size on the page and how easy it is to extract the relevant information for the user. This is dependent on the task type and topic.

These conclusions show that the task type, but also the task topic, has an important influence on user behavior. The task type could influence how users search; the task topic could influence what results are presented by the search engine. The search results could influence dwell times, and nearly all session variables, which in turn could affect the perceived task success and difficulty.

There are lessons for those doing research in interactive IR space. If researchers are using only one topic in their task description, this could greatly influence the results in a free web search task. A good solution for this issue has been applied by Kelly et al. [149] where they used four domains (health, commerce, entertainment, science, and technology) and different topics tailored to study participants as in Borlund's simulated work tasks [45].

3.2   TASK TYPES AND INTENTIONS

A search task can be thought of comprising three vital components: topic (*what*), strategy (*how*), and intent/purpose (*why*). While these three components can be studied at the macro level of a task, one can also examine them at the micro level of a specific action such as a query. Of course, at a query level, the *how* part becomes less visible or certain; we still have the *what* and *why*. We considered the role of the former in the previous section. Now, let us consider the latter.

Intention that is present at a query level is a very important concept to analyze in a search task. In a sense-making interview [85], the information seeker is often asked about their reason or intention behind a particular query or a question. This helps in better understanding the underlying task and providing a personalized solution. Of course, one could do a tautological analysis of a query intention. What is the intention behind the query "rainfall in Sahara"? It is to find out how much rain falls in Sahara. What could be a query if your intention is to find out how much it rains in Sahara? "rainfall in Sahara." In other words, it is easy to think that the intention is clearly expressed in a query. However, many scholars disagree. They see a way and a reason to go deeper into understanding such queries and the intentions behind them.

Some early theoretical research on classifying search sessions could be thought of as applicable to information seeking intentions. For instance, Broder [46] argued that Web searches could be classified into three categories of information seeking and search intention: navigational, transactional, and informational. Aiming to build a more detailed scheme of intentions, Kellar et al. [145] proposed a new typology of user intentions generated in search, which includes fact finding, information gathering, browsing, and transactions. These classifications, as in some later work discussed below, were built upon analysis of queries that initiated search sessions and did not consider the search actions within query segments. Also, these early theoretical classifications only identified broad intention categories and ignored the nuances between different specific intentions within each category.

Besides the theoretical speculation on the classification of intentions, according to Rha et al. [250], Xie [355] is the only example of an empirically based classification of intentions which motivate people to engage in different interactions with search engines. Nevertheless, other similar research on users' goals, knowledge gaps, and search intents can also better help to understand users' intention in information seeking and search episodes. For example, Rose and Levinson [254] analyzed a set of queries randomly selected from AltaVista query logs and proposed a hierarchical typology of users' search goals. Similarly, drawing on the ideas of the sense-making approach [85], Savolainen and Kari [269] revealed the discontinuous and dynamic nature of Web searching episodes and developed a conceptual framework of knowledge gaps faced by searchers as well as the corresponding gap-bridging strategies. Jansen and Booth [128] developed a three-level hierarchy of user intent to automatically classify Web search queries based on the information seeking intentions behind these queries. They found that users' query intent (i.e., informational, navigational, transactional) varies by different search topics.

In recent research on information seeking intention, Mitsui et al. [227] developed a set of information seeking intentions based on the initial typology of interactive intentions [355] and empirically investigated the distributions of different intentions in search tasks of different types. Rha et al. [250] studied how different types and states (i.e., satisfied or unsatisfied) of information seeking intentions lead to different query reformulation strategies. Despite the increasing attention to the role of user intentions, the connections between task, information seeking intentions, and user behavior still has not been systematically studied.

3.2.1   INFORMATION SEEKING INTENTIONS

We will now look at research done by Liu et al. [194] for understanding and extracting information seeking intentions. They used the four tasks—CPE, STP, REL, and INT—listed earlier in this chapter. To classify users' information seeking intentions in web search query segments,

Table 3.2: Information-seeking intentions and the associated acronyms

Categories	Information-Seeking Intentions
Keep record	Keep record of a link (KR)
Identify search information	Identifying something to start (IS); Identify something more to search (IM)
Learn	Learn domain knowledge (LK); Learn database content (LD)
Find	Find known item(s) (FK); Find specific information (FS); Find items sharing a named feature (FN); Find items without predefined criteria (FW)
Access item(s)	Access a specific item (AS); Access items with common characteristics (AC); Access a website/homepage or similar (AW)
Evaluate	Evaluate correctness of an item (EC); Evaluate usefulness of an item (EU); Pick best items from all the useful ones (EB); Evaluate specificity of an item (ES); Evaluate duplication of an item (ED) (i.e., determine whether the information in one item is the same as in others)
Obtain	Obtain specific information to highlight or copy (OS); Obtain part of an item (OP); Obtain a whole item(s) (OW)

their research used the typology of search intentions which was developed and elaborated by Rha et al. [250] based on a subset of Xie's classification of interaction intentions [355]. The authors gave a description of this typology to the participants before their search sessions were replayed for intention annotation. Then, participants were asked to identify their information seeking intention(s) for *each query segment* based on the typology. Participants could identify multiple intentions in the cases where they tried to accomplish multiple things within a single query segment. Details of this process are provided in "Procedures" below. The 20 information seeking intentions are listed in Table 3.2.

3.2.2   EXTRACTING INTENTIONS

The authors conducted a laboratory study to collect the data. This was briefly discussed in the previous section, but now we present the full details. Participants were undergraduate students from Rutgers University, recruited from undergraduate journalism courses. To register, students were required to have completed at least one course in news writing. Each study session consisted of two search tasks, each followed by an annotation task, and several interspersed questionnaires, with a verbal exit interview at the end. All activity except for the exit interview was conducted at a

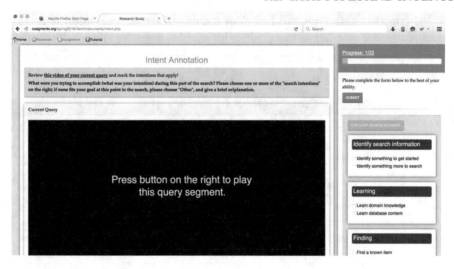

Figure 3.1: Interface for marking search intentions.

desktop computer, with search activity recorded in Firefox by a web browser plugin, eye-fixation behavior by GazePoint,[3] and annotatable video of the search by Morae.[4]

For the intention annotation task, participants were asked to select which intentions applied to each query segment (all that occurred from one query to the next) in the search session. This was accomplished by playing the video of the search, segment by segment. They could select, from a displayed list, any number of intentions for a segment (see Figure 3.1). For instance, if a participant knew nothing about coelacanths and issued the query "coelacanths" as the first query in a session, that person might mark "identify something to get started" and "learn domain knowledge." The participant was then asked to mark whether each of these intentions was satisfied. A participant may mark "yes" for "identify something to get started" but "no" for "learn domain knowledge." If a participant marks "no," she must then state why that intention was not satisfied. For example, while she found some new keywords to search, she may not have learned any knowledge that was required by the task description. If the participant had an unlisted intention, they may also check "other," provide a short description of that additional intention, and also mark whether it was satisfied. They repeated this annotation process for each query segment.

3.2.3   FROM TASK TO INTENTION

To understand the relation between tasks and intentions, the authors performed logistic regression analysis for every information seeking intention. Table 3.3 reports the coefficients of

[3]http://www.gazept.com/
[4]https://www.techsmith.com/morae.html

Table 3.3: The effects of task type and task-user combined features on intentions: Logistic regressions ($*p < .05, **p < 01$; yellow positive effect. blue negative effect. white: no significant effect). IV (independent variable) definitions are in Table 3.4; Table 3.2 defines the intention acronyms (column labels).

IVs	AW	AC	AS	EB	EC	ED	ES	EU	FC	FK	FS	FW	IM	IS	KR	LD	LK	OP	OS	OW
STP	−1.1	−.97	−1.6*	.83*	−.14*	.87	−1.3*	−.33	.03	.10	−.62	.46	.28	−.05	−.68	−.52	.57	−.78	−1.5*	.02
REL	−.28	.84	.22	−.01	−.04	.28	.02	1.1*	1.1	.26	−.14	−.05	1.2*	−.05	−.13	−1.2	1.1*	−.13	−.37	.14
INT	−.84	.12	−.01	−.16	−2.6**	−.58	−.26	−.96	.73	−.36	−.11*	−.50	1.1*	.31	−.69	−.67	.55	−.09	−.76	−.65
QP	−1.9*	.81	1.3	.30	1.3	2.7	1.4	.05	.76	3.5	−3.9	3.5	−.31	−.98*	−.94	−8.6**	2.1	−3.9	3.4	−5.6
TE	.09	−.26	.13	−.04	.45**	−.48**	−.01	.17	−.42**	.03	−.26**	.06	−.47	−.34**	−.17	−.18	−.17	−.22	.07	−.27*
TF	.08	.30*	.09	.02	−.23	.18	.04	−.26*	.53**	.26	.17	−.12	.12	−.29*	.22	.14	.41**	.48**	−.13	−.14
TD	.17	.23	.25	−.14	.35	.29	.22	.33*	.23	.10	.08	.53*	−.01	.09	.36*	−.33	.25	.20	.43**	−.32
TC	.34	.40	.46	.26	.18	.57	.37	.42	.20	.51*	.18	.92*	.15	.21	.52*	−.59	.76**	.49	.69**	.06
STP*QP	.72	.71	1.0	−.85	−.27	−1.7	.83	1.5	−.27	−1.7	−.12	3.9	.14	−1.7	.99	.25	−.58	1.0	1.2	1.5
REL*QP	.79	.57	−.64	.16	−1.1	−.78	.33	2.5*	−.17	−.36	−.03	3.1	−1.5	−.66	−.02	2.2	−.52	.28	.20	.65
INT*QP	.08	.41	−.46	.79	.93	.10	−.07	3.2	−.52	−.28	1.3	4.5	−1.0	−2.1	.90	−.44	−.82	−.42	.15	1.1
TE*QP	−.01	.31	.13	.11	−.61*	.79	−.13	−.45	.34	.48	.19	−.18	.28	−.57	−.17	.17	.09	.30	.05	.67
TF*QP	.25	−.19	.15	.28	.57*	−.36	.22	.64*	−.73*	−.24	−.09	.05	−.13	.61	.06	.04	−.46	−.11	.26	.24
TD*QP	.01	−.74	−.52	−.41	.35	−.79	−.61	−.78*	−.65	−.33	.14	−1.2*	−.13	−.01	−.55	.29	−.09	.25	−.77*	.42
TC*QP	.19	.01	−.04	−.23	.15	−.51	.01	.17	.44	−1.0*	.64	−1.1	.031	.29	.24	1.6	−.34	.36	−.64	.01

different independent variables (IVs) (task type, task-user combined features, query percent, and interaction terms) in each logistic regression model. This model included three binary variables (STP, REL, INT) to represent the categorical variable task type. The copy editing task (CPE) was not explicitly included and thus served as a baseline against which the other task was compared because CPE as a factual specific task has a low level of cognitive complexity [149]. Thus, CPE as a baseline can better help explain the underlying connection between the cognitive demands of different tasks and the frequency of occurrence of different intentions.

Among the reported coefficients, the coefficients of task features can help explain the effects of these variables on the frequency of occurrence of different information seeking intentions. The coefficients of query percent and interaction terms can clarify to what extent the frequency of occurrence of intentions and the main effects of task type and task-user combined features varied across different query segments in search sessions.

From Table 3.3, we can see that the coefficient of query percent is negative and significant in the "AW" column. This indicates that as search session proceeded, participants became less likely to directly go to a website or homepage. This suggests that participants tended to access a knownw website or homepage early in a search session as it could serve as an easy and useful way to kick off the search process and handle the anomalous state of knowledge at the beginning stage. The results in the "AC" column demonstrate that participants with more topic familiarity

Table 3.4: Acronyms of the independent variables in the logistic regressions and the definitions

Acronym	Definition
IV	Independent variable
STP	Story pitch task (binary, Y=1, N=0)
REL	Relationship task (binary, Y=1, N=0)
INT	Interview preparation task (binary, Y=1, N=0)
QP	Query percent
TE	Task familiarity/experience
TF	Topic familiarity
TD	Task difficulty
TC	Time condition
STP*QP	The interaction term between STP and QP
REL*QP	The interaction term between REL and QP
INT*QP	The interaction term between INT and QP
TE*QP	The interaction term between TE and QP
TF*QP	The interaction term between TF and QP
TD*QP	The interaction term between TD and QP
TC*QP	The interaction term between TC and QP

were more likely to access items with common characteristics. This may be because the high level of topic familiarity decreased the difficulty and cognitive load of finding items with common features, and thereby encouraged participants to seek similar items for resolving the tasks. The results in the "AS" column indicate that participants accessed specific known items less frequently in story pitch tasks than in copy editing tasks, indicating that it might be difficult (or not necessary) for participants to use a known item(s) in a factual task without a clearly defined goal.

We now turn our attention to the intentions under the *Evaluate* category. Due to the nature of story pitch task (find web pages which contain the most interesting facts about the topic), participants who conducted this task tended to spend more query segments on picking best item(s) from all the useful ones. The intention of evaluating correctness of an item was affected by both the main effects of task features and an interaction term (task familiarity x query percent). Specifically, when participants were performing the story pitch and interview preparation tasks, they were less likely to evaluate the correctness of retrieved items in query segments since these tasks were open-ended and did not require participants to confirm or disconfirm any statement. Interestingly, the results indicate that higher task familiarity led participants to use significantly more query segments in evaluating correctness. However, as the search sessions proceeded, the effect of task familiarity decreased (i.e., the coefficient of the interaction term is negative). Despite the positive effect on the frequency of occurrence of the intention of evaluating correctness, higher task familiarity was associated with significantly lower frequency of evaluating duplication of the retrieved items. The intention of evaluating specificity appeared less frequently in the story pitch task compared to the "baseline" copy editing task as participants needed to find plenty of relevant, specific items to finish those tasks (confirm or disconfirm the given statements). The results presented in the "EU" column indicate that participants' intention of evaluating usefulness was affected by both task type and task-user combined features (topic familiarity and task difficulty). While the positive effect for the relationship task increased as the search session proceeded, the effects of both topic familiarity and task difficulty gradually decreased over time.

As we consider the intentions under the *Find* category, we find that the frequencies of occurrence of different intentions were associated with different sets of factors. When a participant was more familiar with the task at hand, he or she was less likely to spend time on finding items with something in common. One explanation is that when performing familiar tasks, participants preferred to search for more diversified results and do more explorations, instead of relying on similar websites and documents. In contrast, a high level of topic familiarity encouraged participants to seek similar items. However, the positive effect of topic familiarity decreased as the search session proceeded. When under less time pressure, participants were more likely to spend time on seeking known items. Similar to the aforementioned effect of topic familiarity, this positive effect also decreased over time (the coefficient of the interaction term TC*QP is negative). In terms of the intention of finding specific items, compared to the copy editing task which requires more specific, predefined information, interview preparation is an open-ended task, associated with significantly lower frequency of seeking a predetermined piece of information. In addition, a higher level of task familiarity also was associated with a decrease in the occurrence of the intention of finding specific items. The intention of finding items without predefined criteria frequently happened in tasks with a high level of difficulty as difficult tasks involved more exploratory search activities (without predetermined guidance). In addition, participants who had enough time to work on their tasks were more likely to perform exploratory searches and seek useful web pages without predetermined features. Again, this main effect gradually decreased as the search session proceeded.

Regarding the intentions under *Identify search information* category, participants were more likely to identify something more to search and to explore a topic more broadly in the two open-ended tasks (relationship task and interview preparation task) than in the copy editing task. With respect to the intention of identifying something to get started (e.g., find good query terms), it appeared more frequently in the earlier stages than in the later stages (the coefficient of query percent is negative). Besides, high levels of task familiarity and topic familiarity significantly decreased the frequency of occurrence of this intention, indicating that when a participant was familiar with the task or topic, they were more likely to quickly find useful documents and thus did not need to frequently try and restart new search paths.

Based on results in the "KR" column, when a participant performed a difficult task or had sufficient time in search, they tended to save more useful items to examine later. Regarding the intentions under the *Learn* category, participants tended to learn more about the types of available resources at particular websites in the early stages of search than in later stages. Participants usually spent more query segments on learning domain knowledge in the relationship task than in the copy editing task. Besides, having high levels of topic familiarity or sufficient time in search usually led to higher frequency of seeking domain knowledge.

Finally, with respect to the intentions under the *Obtain* category, when a participant was familiar with the task topic, they were more likely to seek parts of relevant items to highlight or copy. A possible reason is that the familiarity of topic could help them easily locate useful pieces of information within retrieved items. Compared to the baseline situation (copy editing task), participants who were doing the story pitch task were less likely to seek for specific information to highlight or copy. Participants tended to seek specific known items when they experienced higher task difficulty or had relatively sufficient time in search. However, the positive effect of task difficulty tended to decay over time in search sessions. Participants who were doing familiar tasks were less likely to seek a whole item to highlight or copy. This may be because obtaining a whole item is an inefficient way of seeking useful information and thus participants who were familiar with their tasks preferred to avoid this inefficient approach.

3.2.4   FROM INTENTION TO BEHAVIOR

The authors then turned their attention to linking intentions with behaviors. They performed statistical tests for each intention-behavior pair. Table 3.5 illustrates the connection between current search behaviors and current information seeking intentions, and Table 3.6 shows the relationship between current search behaviors and information seeking intentions in the next/subsequent query segment.

Overall, the results in Table 3.5 demonstrate that all intentions identified were significantly associated with at least one aspect of web search in current query segment. In other words, information-seeking intentions were connected to and reflected by web search behavior in various ways. For intentions under *Access* and *Evaluate* categories, they were mostly correlated with click activity, dwell time on SERP, and usefulness judgment behavior. Specifically, when participants had intention(s) related to accessing item(s) or evaluating obtained information, they tended to be more active in browsing, page viewing, and judging the usefulness of gathered information.

In contrast, intention under *Find* category did not show any unified pattern in intention-behavior connection. In other words, different specific intentions in this group were associated with different intentions. For example, the intention of finding information with common features was positively associated with SERP dwell time, as this intention involves evaluating and

Table 3.5: Median of behavioral measure when the intention was selected in *current* query segment. (Mann–Whitney test: *p<.05, **p<.01. yellow: above the mean of total ranks. blue: below the mean of total ranks. white: no significant difference.)

Behavior	AW	AC	AS	EB	EC	ED	ES	EU	FC	FK	FS	FW	IM	IS	KR	LD	LK	OP	OS	OW
query	4	4	4	4	4	3	4	3	4	4	4	3	4	4	4	4	4	4	4	4
click	4	3	4	5	3	6	4	4	3	4	3	3	3	4	3	3	4	3	3.5
source	4	4	4	4	4	5	4	4	4	4	4	4	4	4	5	4	4	4	4	4
page	5	5	5	5	5	8	5	5	5	5	5	5	5	4	6	5	5	5	5	5
SERP	8.2	9.5	7.1	7.9	9.1	4.8	8.4	8.1	7.7	6.2	8.8	7.3	6.7	7.4	8.8	7.5	7.3	12.4	9.6	6.8
content	11.4	11.6	11.8	11.9	11.8	17.7	13.2	13.9	9.5	10.7	11.5	14.0	9.9	11.7	13.9	7.7	12.8	12.4	13.4	14.6
bookmark	1	1	1	1	1	1	1	1	0	1	1	1	0	0	1	0	1	1	1	1

Table 3.6: Median of behavioral measure when the intention was selected in *next* query segment. (Mann-Whitney test: $*p < .05$, $* * p < .01$. yellow: above the mean of total ranks. blue: below the mean of total ranks. white: no significant difference.)

Behavior	AW	AC	AS	EB	EC	ED	ES	EU	FC	FK	FS	FW	IM	IS	KR	LD	LK	OP	OS	OW
query	4	4	4	4	4	4	3	4	4	4	4	3	4	4	4	4	4	4	4	4
click	3	3	3	3.5	3	2	3	3	3	3	3	3	3	3	4	4	4	4	4	4
source	4	4	4	4	4	4	4	4	4	4	4	4	4	5	4	4	4	4	4	4
page	5	5	5	5	5	5	5	5	5	5	5	5	5	5	5	5	5	5	5	5
SERP	6.5	6.8	7.0	5.8	7.1	9.2	6.2	6.3	7.1	6.0	6.9	7.4	5.6	6.0	6.8	6.7	5.8	6.9	7.3	6.0
content	12.1	10.2	11.1	10.5	11.3	7.2	10.5	10.7	10.1	9.1	10.3	15.3	9.7	12.2	11.9	9.4	11.3	11.3	11.3	13.7
bookmark	1	1	1	1	1	0	0	1	1	0	0	1	0	1	1	1	1	1	0	1

comparing results on SERPs. However, the intention of finding specific information was more closely correlated with content page viewing and usefulness judgment behaviors. With respect to the *Identify* category, participants tended to leave SERPs earlier when they merely wanted to identify something more to search, rather than deeply examine the results. When participants sought to identify a starting point for web search, they were more active in content page reading and clicking, but less patient with SERP viewing and visiting more pages.

Similar to the intentions in *Access* and *Evaluate* groups, most of the intentions under *Keep*, *Learn* and *Obtain* categories were also closely related to clicking, content page viewing, and bookmarking behaviors, indicating that intentions under these categories could lead to similar search tactics. Among these intentions, when participants sought to learn domain knowledge, they tended to spend less time on browsing SERPs but much longer time on carefully reading the clicked content pages. The intentions of learning database information and obtaining a whole item(s) were only associated with one of the search behaviors, suggesting that their connections to web search might be loose. Another possible reason is the small sample size. Neither of these two intentions occurred frequently (frequencies both below than 15%), limiting our ability to fully determine the connections between intentions and behaviors.

The authors found that compared to the rich connections between search behavior and current intentions, fewer significant associations were discovered between search behavior and subsequent intentions (see Table 3.6). Among all types of intentions, seven intentions had no significant connection with search behavior. This result indicates that some of the intentions were more closely restricted to the local steps or micro-situation (i.e., query segment) and were loosely connected (if not totally disconnected) with previous actions. For other intentions, most of them were positively associated with click activity and usefulness judgments (i.e., bookmarking) behaviors.

3.3 SUMMARY

This chapter demonstrated that task is not an isolated construct in IR, nor should it be studied that way. In fact, it is a very important realization for us as we will expand on in the next two chapters that task is intrinsically and meaningfully connected to user behaviors, their intentions, and task performance or outcome.

In this chapter, through various case studies, we observed how scholars have investigated the effects of task types on user behaviors and intentions. Often, these scholars have also used what they could observe (e.g., user activity) to derive the nature of the task, assuming that those behaviors are being affected by the underlying task. In the next chapter, we will see this approach in more detail as we examine case studies that use behavioral and other signals to explicate task information.

CHAPTER 4

Explicating Task

While many scholars argue and almost all agree that there is a task behind information seeking activities, it is not always clear what that task is. Asking the searcher for that task is not always possible or advisable. In this chapter, we discuss how researchers have found ways to explicate that task knowledge from other signals. We will start with a clear case of task being expressed by the user—not because a scholar is asking, but because the users want to do so.

4.1 USING EXPLICITLY EXPRESSED TASKS

While recognizing implicit tasks is an important avenue for research, we overlook the fact that people do express their tasks explicitly—only that this happens outside the search system—typically in to-do applications (e.g., Google Tasks, Microsoft To Do). We ask the question: can we analyze those tasks and identify the ones appropriate for search systems? And if we can, what is the likelihood that the task expression (typically a short phrase such as "order contact lens") can map directly to a search query? We performed a study that sought out to answer these questions to bridge the explicit expression of to-do tasks and web search [280].

4.1.1 DATA

We started with an anonymized, aggregated subset of tasks appearing in the now-defunct Wunderlist task management application. The application had a default task list, to which tasks were added if the user did not specify a specific list. We wanted to focus on tasks where the intent was clear from the text of the task titles only. Tasks titles appearing in non-default lists often rely on the list name to provide context, e.g., the "milk" example in the grocery list, where the intent is clearly to buy milk (and not watch the movie by the same name) even though that it not explicitly stated. From the default list, we needed to remove the tasks that either did not have a leading verb that indicate an action to take and/or the context was very clear. For example, the task "call mom" would not be considered because it was clearly a task that had an assigned context (phone). We ordered these tasks by their frequency to identify top action verbs in the default list. The authors reviewed the top 50 most frequent tasks manually and selected verbs that could have a context outside of strongly indicative action terms such as phone/call, email, print, and clean. The resultant set of verbs considered to identify suitable tasks for this analysis were: *book, bring, buy, change, check, collect, find, finish, fix, get, look, make, move, order, pay, pick, post, put, renew, reschedule, return, sell, send, set, submit, take, update.*

Using this subset of selected action verbs, we filtered the aggregated tasks data and identified a set of tasks that: (1) started with one of these verbs; (2) were added to the default list; and (3) appeared in the task lists of 100 or more users of the Wunderlist application. This generated a total of 7,563 unique task titles. We sorted these in descending order by user frequency and selected the top 1,000 task titles for human annotation.

4.1.2   ANALYSIS

As we analyzed the 1,000 tasks annotated by the 5 judges, we found that some tasks clearly fit 1 of 4 categories—offline, online, search, and unclear—with all judges assigning the same label, whereas some of them had a majority label (3 or 4 out of 5 judges picked the same category). Out of 5,000 total judgments, only 20 were marked as "Unclear." In almost all the cases, the reason given was "insufficient information or context." For the task "book review," all five judges marked it as "Unclear." Two other tasks worth noticing were "book group" (4 out of 5 marking as "Unclear") and "check out" (3 out of 5 marking as "Unclear"). In all three cases, there are multiple interpretations of the task title and contextual/personal knowledge is required to understand the task.

We then investigated the aggregated judgments for the tasks, as grouped by the leading verbs, e.g., when a task starts with "buy," 86% of the time the judges marked it for "search." We also studied how often the tasks with the leading verb obtains the label using majority voting, e.g., tasks starting with "book" get the "Online" label 76% of the time through majority voting. Table 4.1 lists the results for all verbs. In that table, "Aggregated label" and $P(A)$ indicate the most common label for all tasks prefixed with the given verb and the corresponding probability in the dataset. Similarly, "Majority label" and $P(M)$ indicate how often tasks with the given verb as a prefix received a label as selected by most judges.

We found that for around 60% of the verbs considered here, we are able to predict whether a task is suitable for offline, online, or search with high confidence. The verbs that were most unclear ($p < 0.5$) were "change" and "sell." Upon examining the data, it appeared that the confusion for "change" tasks lay between whether these tasks should be completed offline or online. We found that this depended on the noun that followed "change." For example, the task "change bed" is suitable for offline, whereas "change dentist appointment" is more suitable for online. Based on this insight, we hypothesized that if the noun is tangible (e.g., bed, oil filter), the task would fall under "offline," whereas if the noun is abstract (e.g., password, appointment, address), the task would fall under "online." In contrast, the inter-judge disagreement for "sell" tasks was between online and search, suggesting that the utility of search in selling something was unclear.

Interestingly, while "buy" tasks were very clearly marked for search, only 52% times "order" tasks obtained a majority vote for search. Here also, the confusion lay between the "online" and the "search" labels. We believe that this confusion may be due to the perceived intentions behind these two verbs: "buy" may be perceived as still tentative and thus benefiting from search, whereas "order" may indicate a resolved intention that is at a more advanced state and hence may

Table 4.1: Task starting verbs with their labels by either aggregating or majority vote, and their corresponding probabilities

Verb	Agg. Label	$P(A)$	Maj. Label	$P(M)$
book	online	0.72	online	0.76
bring	offline	0.98	offline	1.00
buy	search	0.86	search	0.86
change	offline	0.50	offline	0.51
check	online	0.55	online	0.62
collect	offline	1.00	offline	1.00
find	search	0.74	search	0.71
finish	offline	0.54	offline	0.50
fix	offline	0.90	offline	0.88
get	offline	0.60	offline	0.54
look	search	0.75	search	0.75
make	offline	0.62	offline	0.63
move	offline	0.90	offline	0.86
order	search	0.52	search	0.66
pay	online	0.98	online	0.98
pick	offline	0.96	offline	1.00
post	offline	0.55	offline	0.69
put	offline	1.00	offline	1.00
renew	online	0.97	online	1.00
reschedule	online	0.96	online	1.00
return	online	0.76	online	0.85
sell	online	0.47	online	0.64
send	online	0.82	online	0.85
set	offline	0.67	offline	0.63
submit	online	0.97	online	1.00
take	offline	1.00	offline	1.00
update	online	0.89	online	0.95

or may not need help from a search engine. This hypothesis can easily be tested in follow on studies by asking judges to annotate the same noun with a different start verb, such as "buy dog food" and "order dog food."

4.1.3   A SIMPLE RULE-BASED ALGORITHM FOR TASK LABELING

Based on our analysis and observations, we devised a simple algorithm (see Algorithm 4.1) to assign a task "offline," "online," or "search" labels. Applying this algorithm to our data (1,000 tasks), we obtain 82% accuracy if we consider aggregated labels as the ground truth. If we consider majority labels, on the other hand, the accuracy increases to 84%. Note that if we do further refinement of our crude rules, as with the last two cases above, we could potentially get higher accuracies.

Algorithm 4.1 : Task Classification.

Input: Task titles/phrases
Output: Class label
    Initialize label='unknown'
1: **if** the task starts with verbs *collect, put, take, bring, pick, fix, move, set, make, get, finish* **then**
    label = 'offline'
2: **end if**
3: **if** the task starts with verbs *pay, renew, submit, reschedule, update, send, return, book, check, sell* **then**
    label = 'online'
4: **end if**
5: **if** the task starts with verbs *buy, look, find, order* **then**
    label = 'search'
6: **end if**
7: **if** the task starts with verbs *change*, followed by a tangible noun **then**
    label = 'online'
8: **end if**
9: **if** the task starts with verbs *post*, followed by an online service **then**
    label = 'online'
10: **else**
    label = 'offline'
11: **end if**

Table 4.2: Frequencies of tasks per category from the Bing query log over a three-week (non-contiguous) time period. Tasks are matched to queries in their original forms, with preceding verbs removed, and "amazon" tasks removed as outliers.

| Category | Tasks | Original | | Preceding Verbs Removed | | 'Amazon' Tasks Removed | |
		Query Freq	Avg Freq	Query Freq	Avg Freq	Query Freq	Avg Freq
Offline	405	8,932	22.11	8,932	22.11	8,932	22.11
Online	366	21,283	58.15	21,283	58.15	21,283	58.15
Search	229	6,390	27.90	9,815,280	42,861.48	2,237,024	9,768.66

4.1.4   CONNECTING TASKS WITH SEARCHES

Next, we examined how the actionable tasks from Wunderlist show up in queries issued to the Bing web search engine. Specifically, we took those 1,000 tasks and looked for exact matches in Bing logs over three non-contiguous weeks in 2020. The "Original" columns in Table 4.2 present the results. The "Tasks" column indicates how many tasks were in each category. "Query freq" describes the aggregated frequency of queries that match with the tasks. "Avg freq" describes "Query freq" divided by "Tasks."

As we can see, the offline tasks do not appear as frequently in the search logs. However, search-friendly tasks do not seem to appear often either. This may be because people do not pose their to-do tasks verbatim to search engines, e.g., for the task "buy bus tickets," the corresponding search query would likely be "bus tickets." When we match the tasks with the search queries after removing "buy," "order," and "find" from the task titles, we obtain a huge spike in search-friendly task matches. The new statistics are shown in the "Preceding verbs removed" columns in Table 4.2. The task "order amazon" appeared in the tasks data and "amazon" (the matching query following the removal of "order") is a highly popular, navigational query in the logs. We removed those queries as outliers.

Table 4.2 shows that tasks that our algorithm determined to be search-friendly are indeed very likely to appear in search engines. In order to further verify this, we ranked the matched queries in descending order by their frequency. Then, we computed reciprocal rank (RR) and weighted RR (WRR) for each of the three categories (online, offline, and search) as follows:

$$RR_{category} = \sum \frac{1}{rank_i} \qquad \text{where } label(i) = category \qquad (4.1)$$

$$WRR_{category} = \sum freq(i) \cdot \frac{1}{rank_i} \quad \text{where } label(i) = category. \qquad (4.2)$$

We then took the averages across all the queries in a given class for RR and WRR to compute mean values of MRR and MWRR (see Table 4.3). Here, the higher MRR indicates the results in that class are at higher ranks based on their frequency in the search logs. The "search"

Table 4.3: Mean reciprocal rank (MRR) and mean weighted MRR (MWRR) by label

	MRR	MWRR
Offline	0.0019	0.1119
Online	0.0022	0.8401
Search	0.0256	2826.3230

labeled tasks have queries matching much higher ranks than those with "online" and certainly "offline." When we weigh these ranks with their corresponding frequencies using MWRR, we observe that the tasks identified as "search-friendly" tasks are indeed the highest ranked and most prominent queries among all task-related queries. Users are clearly already using search engines for the tasks we identified as "search-friendly" more so than for other types of tasks, providing another form of validation for our results.

4.1.5   ANALYZING UNMATCHED SEARCH TASKS

Not all tasks that were labeled suitable for search showed up in Bing logs. Of course, the simplest explanation is that we only analyzed a sample of Bing logs over a limited period of time. A longer duration or a larger sample may have yielded matches for all these tasks. Nonetheless, looking at the search tasks that did not find a query match, we found that two thirds were "buy" tasks. Nine items were "order" tasks, five were "find" tasks, and two were "look at/for" tasks.

Once we removed the prefixes "buy," "order," and "find" from task titles and looked for query matches, we were left with only a small number of unmatched search tasks. Almost all the non-matching items were actual objects that people did not search for in our sampled log. Not all purchasing activities come through search engines. In some cases, users may go directly to specialized e-commerce services. Two exceptions were "look at/for" tasks, whose prefixes should also be removed when matching with historic queries as these tasks are clear candidates for searching.

4.1.6   IMPLICATIONS FOR SEARCH ENGINES

This study provided compelling evidence that we can identify search-friendly tasks from to-do lists. While almost any task can be linked to a search engine, to gain user trust and help ensure the usability of this proposed functionality, IR systems should only provide such a link for tasks with high confidence. Considering this, we provide the following recommendation for the overall flow of such a "task-to-search" functionality, which could be offered in task management systems.

1. For a given item in one's to-do list, identify whether or not it is actionable (as in [347]).

2. For this actionable item, use the algorithm given here or more sophisticated machine-learned variant to identify whether it is suitable for offline, online, or search.

3. If the task item is deemed to be search-friendly, create a link to a search engine and provide it with the item on the interface in the task management system.

In addition to continuing to work with these steps, we are also considering tasks requiring multiple queries by analyzing *sessions* instead of individual queries in the search logs. This becomes quite important as we acknowledge and address the fact that many tasks are not accomplished using single queries or even a collection of queries directly executed on a search engine. To truly address the underlying tasks, one needs to contextualize and perhaps expand its meaning and then consider how or if search can help. A part of this contextualization can also be achieved by considering various attributes around a task's expression such as time, place, other tasks entered at the same time, and a user's own background and profile.

4.2 DERIVING TASK FROM USER BEHAVIORS

Now we will see efforts for learning about the underlying task when it is not expressed explicitly like in the previous section. The most common way to derive task information in such a case is using various forms of user behavior. This is based on a well-founded assumption that the task affects people's behaviors, and if we make appropriate observations about those behaviors, we could explicate that task.

In the past decade, we have seen many works along this line, several of them summarized in Chapter 2. There are two main reasons for such an increased attention to this research: (1) it has become progressively easier to collect large amounts of behavioral data as the tools for collecting them have been widely developed and deployed even for academic communities (e.g., [223, 289]); and (2) new techniques have been developed that allow more sophisticated connection of users, their tasks, and their behaviors. Given that a lot of relevant literature has been covered before, here we will go into some depths of these two points with three case studies—the first two show how user behavior data can be used for identifying task stages and the third one shows how we could develop a comprehensive model of an interactive IR process using user, task, and behavior information.

4.2.1 QUERY-RELATED BEHAVIORS FOR TASK TYPE PREDICTION

Mitsui et al. [224] started with a simple question—*given a searcher's behavior during a search session, can the searcher's task be predicted?* Of course, even if we could do this using the behavioral data from the whole session, is that really useful? What is the point of predicting task type after the task is done? Therefore, the authors also asked if they could do this using very little data—just the data associated with the first query—from a session.

For this, the authors chose to predict the goal and product of the task, in the sense defined by Li and Belkin [183]. The goal is a binary classification of "specific" or "amorphous," analogous to the well-defined or ill-defined goals in [126]. The product is either "intellectual"—producing new findings, or "factual"—locating facts or data. These task types are largely dependent on a task specification that can be controlled by an experimenter. Moreover, pairing these products and goals yields four possible task types: "known-fact search" ("factual"/"specific"), "known-subject search" ("factual"/"amorphous"), "interpretive search" ("intellectual"/"specific"), and "exploratory search" ("intellectual"/"amorphous").

Their first dataset was the TREC 2014 Session Track [62], which has been used in the evaluation of retrieval over the course of a search session. This data is comprised of search logs of users conducting searches over sessions, rather than performing ad hoc retrieval. The data has 1,257 sessions, with 260 unique users conducting searches across 60 different topics (15 unique prompts per task type). The authors used 1,021 of these sessions; the others do not include a current or final query and cannot be applied for their work. The searchers in the TREC data were recruited through MTurk. In contrast, their second data was from the previously described study in Chapter 3 [227]. As a reminder, the participants were undergraduate journalism student and were given journalism-based task prompts across four task types following the same faceted classification: copy editing (factual/specific), story pitch (factual/amorphous), relationships (intellectual/amorphous), interview preparation (intellectual/amorphous). There were 80 sessions total: 22 copy editing, 18 story pitch, 18 relationships, and 22 interview preparation. Forty participants conducted 2 sessions each.

The authors predicted the task type (goal and product) using either first query features or whole session features listed below. They performed traditional machine learning (ML) classification experiments, with the task product, goal, or type of a session as the classification label. Hence, they had 1,021 total data points and 80 data points for the TREC and journalism data, respectively. The TREC data contained 513 amorphous tasks, 508 specific tasks, 529 factual tasks, and 492 intellectual tasks. The journalism data contained 58 amorphous tasks, 22 specific tasks, 40 factual tasks, and 40 intellectual tasks. The authors compared several ML classifiers against two naive baselines. For both datasets, they used 80% training data and 20% test data.

While a rich set of features can be extracted from a controlled laboratory study, the authors limited themselves to the first query and the whole session features that could be extracted from both the TREC 2014 Session Track data and journalism data, to come as close to creating a genuine replication as possible. Since they were examining the effects of first query and whole session features in task type prediction, they used the same features in their two experiments on the two datasets. The features are as follows.

First query features

- Query length, total dwell time on SERPs and content pages, percentage of time on SERPs. These are directly drawn or derived from [12], and associated with differences between task types.

- Number of pages visited. This is a specific case of the number of pages visited over a session [191].

Whole session features

- Number of pages, number of queries, and completion time. These distinguish task types in [191].

- Dwell time on content pages per SERP, percentage of time on SERPs, dwell time on SERP per query, dwell time on content pages per query, total dwell time on SERP pages, total dwell time on content pages. These are directly drawn from or derived from [134].

- Average dwell time on content pages, pages per query, average query length, range of query lengths.

Their results show the following three simple conclusions.

1. **Prediction with first query features can be more accurate than with whole session features.** This happened in all cases in both datasets excepting only the task goal in the journalism data. In that case, the whole session features obtained 0.738 accuracy vs. 0.715 accuracy for first query features.

2. **Additionally, first query features can be significantly more accurate.** This happened for task product in both datasets ($p < .01$), providing strong evidence that first query features are generally better for predicting whether a product is factual or intellectual. This only happened once with goal and once with task type in the TREC dataset ($p < .01$).

3. **If #1 or #2 above do not hold, whole session features are still not significantly more accurate than first query features.** The result for task goal in the journalism data (an accuracy of 0.738 for the whole session vs. 0.715 for the first query only), violated #1. Similarly for first query features on task type (accuracy is 0.5 for the whole session vs. 0.501 for first query only). In both cases, the best whole session predictor was not significantly better than the best first query predictor, despite differences.

4.2.2 IDENTIFYING TASK STAGES

As we saw in Chapter 1, a task can be thought of as consisting multiple levels or stages [52, 53]. Knowing which of this levels or stages the user is working currently can be instrumental in providing personalized support. Therefore, we will now look at a case study by Liu et al. [195] for identifying task stages using behavioral signals.

The authors used data from two controlled laboratory studies, *information seeking intention* (ISI) study [222] and *problem-help* (PH) study [267]. ISI study explored users' information seeking intentions and search actions in different query segments of complex search tasks, and PH study investigated the association between users' encountered problems, help needed, as well as their search behavior. Analyzing the empirical evidence collected from these two studies enabled us to characterize and model the states of complex search tasks from different perspectives.

The data collected from ISI and PH studies enabled the authors to model the states of complex search tasks from active aspect and situational, unanticipated aspect, respectively. In the datasets, each intention, problem, and help item was represented using a unique binary variable (present=1, absent=0). For state identification, we used *K-modes clustering analysis* for extracting clusters out of user annotation data. K-modes clustering as a unsupervised learning method extends the traditional K-means paradigm to cluster categorical data [66]. In the clustering analysis, different information seeking intentions, in-situ problems, and types of help needed were considered as separate elements within the vectors representing unique task states.

To test the validity of the task state categories extracted from annotation data, the authors ran *external judgment of state types* with two external assessors. Specifically, they randomly extracted 10% of searches from each type of tasks and ask the two assessors to manually annotate task state for each query segment independently according to the task states they extracted and defined. Each assessor was provided with the video of participants' search process, the intention or problem-help annotation and search behavior data, as well as the state typology generated by the K-modes clustering algorithm. To measure the validity of task state labels, the authors computed three *Cohen's Kappa coefficients*, between (1) the two annotators, (2) the annotator *A* and the clustering algorithm, and (3) the annotator *B* and the clustering algorithm. To ensure the quality of task state labeling and judgment, they recruited two advanced Ph.D. students majoring in IR as their external assessors.

The identification of task states started with K-modes clustering analysis. Prior to that, the authors employed the average silhouette method to determine the optimal number of clusters. They extracted four clusters as separate task states from the ISI dataset and six clusters from the PH dataset. The clustering analysis for PH study was conducted based on 216 query segments as the problem-help annotation was missing for some of the repeated queries due to system errors.

Focusing on the active, intention aspect of task state, the authors identified the following four states of complex search tasks. They interpreted each extracted task state based on the main (most frequent) information seeking intentions within the state.

- **Exploitation** (frequency: 54.3%, 376 query segments): The two most frequent intentions are *find specific information* (39.4%) and *identify something more to search* (40.4%). Meanwhile, the intention of identifying something to start searching never occurs. In this state, users may have a clear topic in mind and they try to follow the current search path, keep exploiting the information patch at hand and search for more relevant pages.

- **Known-Item** (frequency: 18.2%, 126 query segments): The two most frequent intentions are *find specific information* (100%) and *obtain specific information items* (100%). In this state, users may have very specific, well-defined information need(s) or item(s) in mind.

- **Exploratory** (frequency: 16.6%, 115 query segments): The most frequent intention in this state is identify something to start searching (100%). In this state, users may try to adopt new search strategies, explore unknown subtopics, or open new search paths.

- **Learn and Evaluate** (frequency: 10.9%, 76 query segments): In this state, most intentions under the *Evaluate* category (above 60%) and the intentions of learning domain knowledge and keeping useful links (both above 80%) occurred frequently.

Similarly, with respect to the situational (problem-help) aspect of task state, the authors identified six task states and explained them based upon the most frequent search problem(s) and/or help needed. They used acronyms to represent each state here as it is difficult to assign any meaningful label to cover all traits of these problem-help states.

- **IO-P** (frequency: 21.3%, 46 query segments): The most frequently occurring problem was information overload (IO) (34.8%) and main type of help needed was web page (P) recommendation (74%).

- **ASK-LT-PE** (frequency: 11.6%, 25 query segments): In this state, users were very likely to experience the anomalous state of knowledge [28] (ASK: do not know how to express their information need or what exactly they are looking for) (64%) and other barriers, such as lack of topic knowledge (LT) (72%) and not knowing potentially useful information sources (64%). In this state, they usually prefer to have people (PE) who can guide them through the search process.

- **ASK-SU-M** (frequency: 11.6%, 25 query segments): In this state, users were very likely to encounter the ASK issue (76%) and the problem of not knowing useful sources (80%). Here, users often preferred to have multiple types of supports, such as page recommendation (88%), query recommendation (96%), and strategy recommendation (92%).

- **NP** (frequency: 36.1%, 78 query segments): In this state, users often had no explicit search problem (NP) (70%) and thus did not need any specific help from the search system (88.6%).

- **LT-M** (frequency: 4.6%, 10 query segments): In this state, the problem of lacking topic knowledge frequently occurs (89%) and users needed multiple types of help, such as page recommendation (89%), people recommendation (89%), and search strategy recommendation (100%).

- **SU-QU** (frequency: 14.8%, 32 query segments): In this state, users were very likely to encounter the problem of not knowing useful information sources (63%) and usually prefered to have useful query recommendations from the system (75%).

Table 4.4: Behavioral variations across different intention-based task states: median (IQR) (*: p<.05, **: p<.01)

Behavior	Exploit	Known	Eplore	Learn	Dunn's Posthoc Test
querylength*	4(3)	4(3)	3(4)	3(3)	E>EX*,K>EX*,E>L*,K>L*
dwellSERP**	7.2(10)	7.3(10)	6.2(7)	4.9(3)	K>EX*,E>L*,K>L**
dwcontent**	7.9(14)	13.5(15)	8.9(17)	13(15.9)	K>E*,K>EX*,L>E*,L>EX*
N.content**	5(2)	4(3)	4(4)	3(2)	E>L*,K>L*
totalcontent**	33(69)	67(92)	35(28)	54(83)	K>E*,K>EX*,L>E*,L>EX*
N.clicks**	2(3)	3(4)	3(4)	4.5(5.5)	L>E**,L>EX*,L>K*,EX>E*
N.bookmark**	0(1)	0(1)	0(1)	1(2)	L>E*,L>K*,L>EX*

To test the validity of the above task states extracted by K-modes clustering algorithm, the authors invited two assessors to do manual task state annotation and computed the Cohen's Kappa coefficients κ for all three pairs: (1) annotator A and annotator B: 0.782 (ISI-based state), 0.768 (PH-based state); (2) annotator A and clustering algorithm: 0.716 (ISI-based state), 0.717 (PH-based state); and (3) annotator B and clustering algorithm: 0.744 (ISI-based state), 0.682 (PH-based state). The Cohen's Kappa agreements in all pairs are above 0.65, which is considered *substantial* agreement [172]. This high level of agreement demonstrates that the task state typology generated by the clustering algorithm is reliable and can be used for further analysis. Also, it is worth noting that neither of the between-annotator agreements crossed the threshold of "almost perfect" agreement (0.8) [172], indicating that inferring implicit task states from search interactions is not an easy job (even for human annotators).

To further explore the boundaries between task states, the authors examined the extent to which the identified states differ from each other in terms of the associated search behaviors. Table 4.4 presents the results of statistical tests on the behavioral variation across different intention-based task states. In general, when participants had a relatively clear topic or specific item in mind (in exploitation or known-item states), they tended to issue longer, more specific queries and spend more time on seeking the most relevant information directly on SERPs. In contrast, when participants were in a learning and evaluation state, they tended to stay longer on content pages and perform more clicks and bookmarks (for usefulness judgments). These results demonstrate that the intention-based task states are closely associated with participants' selections of search tactics in local search steps.

Table 4.5 illustrates the behavioral variations across different problem-help states. The results indicate that when participants encountered the problems of ASK and lacking topic knowledge (ASK-LT-PE), they tended to be more active in browsing SERPs and reading content pages, seeking to find useful cues for formulating queries and selecting correct search paths. When participants encountered the information overload problem (IO-P), they were likely to

Table 4.5: Behavioral variations across different problem-help-based task states (*: p<.05, **: p<.01)

Behavior	Dunn's Posthoc Test
querylength*	ASK-SU-M>IO-P**, ASK-LT-PE*, NP*, SU-QU*
dwellSERP**	ASK-LT-PE>IO-P**, NP**,LT-M*, SU-OU*;ASK-SU-M>NP*, SU-OU**
dwcontent	N.A.
N.content*	ASK-LT-PE>IO-P*, ASK-SU-M*, NP*, SU-QU*; ASK-SU-M>NP*
totalcontent**	ASK-LT-PE>IO-P*, ASK-SU-M*, NP*, LT-M*, SU-QU*
N.clicks**	IO-P>ASK-SU-M*; ASK-LT-PE>ASK-SU-M*, LT-M*, SU-QU*
N.bookmark**	NP>ASK-LT-PE**, ASK-SU-M*, LT-M*, SU-QU*

be distracted by many (irrelevant) information items, which resulted in more clicking actions. In contrast, when participants had no explicit search problem, they tended to bookmark more useful pages, indicating that they were on the right track of searching.

4.2.3   BUILDING A COMPREHENSIVE MODEL USING INFORMATION ABOUT TASKS, USERS, AND THEIR BEHAVIORS

Now that we have seen how task types affect intentions and user behaviors, it is time to ask how it all relates. Most studies we have seen—either while reviewing the relevant literature in Chapter 2 or in the presentation of various case studies—were focused on studying or establishing a connection between user behaviors and intentions, or task types and behaviors, or task types and intentions. However, in an information interaction episode, all of these are happening together, with one aspect possibly affecting all others. For instance, a user's background (e.g., novice, subject expert) may affect how difficult they perceive a given task to be, and that in turn may affect their behaviors.

To expand our views on user behaviors, intentions, and task types, we will now consider a model that could give us a comprehensive understanding of how all of these relate to one another. We will do that not simply to better explain these constructs in context, but also as a way to make better, more nuanced predictions involving user behaviors and tasks. Specifically, we will look at the work by Mitsui and Shah [225], which attempted to create such a comprehensive model— primarily as a theoretical construct, but then also applying to some datasets—using path analysis and developing a structural equation model (SEM).

There are two methods to developing path models and SEMs. The first begins with exploratory factor analysis to discover the optimal number of latent variables in a SEM and the strengths of relationships between variables. This is followed by confirming the model's goodness of fit on external or held-out data. Such an approach was taken to model relationships between document reliability, understandability, topicality, novelty, and scope [371].

The second approach is to build a model from literature review. Significant relationships between variables from literature indicate dependencies/equations in the model. This approach has been taken in works such as that of Khakurel et al. [155]. Since much of the relevant literature has explored the relationship between task, topic, browser signals, and other user characteristics, the authors adopted the latter approach, later examining their findings for confirming evidence of their model choice.

Below, the authors list all relationships included in their model (as directed and two-way arrows). They also identified citations for relationships where significant differences have been found, taking the opportunity to list additional relationships to test. All of these features were included in their most complex path model, as discussed in the next subsection.

- **Exogenous variables**: Task goal, task product, topic, and *Background* variables.

- **Behaviors/Signals**: Number of pages viewed, total content page dwell time, total SERP dwell time, and query length for a query segment.

- **Task → Behaviors**: Task goal, product → *Behaviors* [12, 134, 191].

- **Task → Intentions → Behaviors**: Task goal, product → intention groups [227]; intention groups→*Behaviors* [222].

- **Task/Topic → Search Experience**: Task product, goal → search difficulty [193]; Topic → topic familiarity.

- **Background → Search Experience**: Search years → search difficulty; Search frequency → search difficulty.

- **Background → Intentions**: Search expertise → intentions [209, 250].

- **Experience → Behaviors**: Topic familiarity → *Behaviors* [119, 192]; Search difficulty → *Behaviors* [11, 13, 192].

- **Within-category Correlations**: Adequate time ⟷ task difficulty [81]; Assignment experience ⟷ search difficulty [193]; Task goal ⟷ task product; Topic familiarity → search difficulty.

See Figure 4.1 for a summary of the full model. Each node of the model indicates several variables. For instance, the "Task" node indicates three binary variables: the task goal, the task product, and the task category. And a path indicates that there is some dependency between them. Also note that henceforth we use "Behaviors" and "Signals" interchangeably.

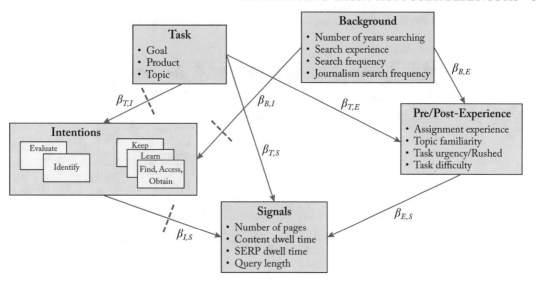

Figure 4.1: The full path model used in Mitsui and Shah's [225] analyses. Blue paths indicate all connections used in the full path model. The red dotted lines indicate paths that are omitted when intentions are omitted from analysis.

Model Variations

A path analysis begins with two basic models: the *saturated* model and *independent* model. The saturated model assumes that all variables are correlated with each other. That is, when given n variables there are $\frac{n(n+1)}{2}$ paths. The independent model, in contrast, assumes no variables are connected to each other and that variables' values are only manifest through their error variance.

These two models are compared to the models the researcher creates. The model constructed in the previous section is considered as the *full model*. The authors derived several models from the full model as follows: (1) select categories of variables $C_{excl} = \{C_1, ..., C_n\}$ (e.g., {*Background*, *Experience*}); and (2) select edges from C_{excl} that would directly or indirectly connect it to task properties or browser signals, and constrain the edges to 0. Figure 4.1, in addition to showing the full figure, shows an example which disconnects the *Intentions* from task and signals. In addition to its direct connections, its connection to background is also severed so that it does not influence the background variables.

One could remove variables from the path model entirely, but the evaluation metrics for path analysis are relative to the saturated model, dependent on the covariance matrix, and therefore dependent on the number of variables. The authors, therefore, constrained path values as above. See Table 4.6 for a summary of these variations.

Table 4.6: The different models tested, as well as whether there are edges between each group (Y=Yes, N=No)

Model Name	$\beta_{T,E}$	$\beta_{T,I}$	$\beta_{B,E}$	$\beta_{B,I}$	$\beta_{E,S}$	$\beta_{I,S}$	$\beta_{T,S}$
Full Model	Y	Y	Y	Y	Y	Y	Y
IB	N	Y	N	Y	N	Y	Y
IE	Y	Y	N	N	Y	Y	Y
I	N	Y	Y	N	N	Y	Y
BE	Y	N	Y	N	Y	N	Y
E	Y	N	N	Y	Y	N	Y
Task Only	N	N	Y	Y	N	N	Y

Evaluation Metrics

As a part of evaluation, it is reasonable to ask: how important is each variable category in affecting task and/or behaviors? In path analysis, this is equivalent to: how well do different path constraints explain covariance in the data? The data supplied to path analysis is a covariance matrix. That is, a square matrix Σ where each index Σ_{ij} is:

$$\Sigma_{ij} = E[(X_i - \mu_i)(X_j - \mu_j)].\tag{4.3}$$

Evaluation metrics for path models are largely based on goodness of fit, with respect to recapturing Σ. The saturated model recreates this covariance matrix perfectly, while other models create an imperfect covariance matrix S. A fundamental evaluation metrics χ^2, which compares S to Σ:

$$\chi^2 = \sum_{ij} \frac{(S_{ij} - \Sigma_{ij})^2}{\Sigma_{ij}}.\tag{4.4}$$

A similar metric is the goodness of fit index (GFI)

$$GFI = 1 - \frac{Cov_{residual}}{Cov_{total}},\tag{4.5}$$

where Cov_{total} is the total covariance of S and $Cov_{residual}$ is leftover covariance from the error terms; higher scores are better.

Other scores adjust in favor of model simplicity. These penalize based on degrees of freedom, number of parameters, or the number of data points. Two such are the adjusted GFI (AGFI) and parsimonious GFI (PGFI). Another popular one, the root mean squared error (RMSEA), is provided by:

$$RMSEA = \sqrt{\frac{\chi^2 - df}{df(N - 1)}}.\tag{4.6}$$

Last, the Aikake information criterion (AIC) and Bayesian information criterion (BIC) are provided as follows:

$$AIC = \chi^2 + k(k + 1) + 2df \tag{4.7}$$

$$BIC = \chi^2 + \ln(N)\left(\frac{k(k + 1)}{2} - df\right), \tag{4.8}$$

where N is the number of data points, k is the number of parameters and df is the number of degrees of freedom.

Results

The authors compared the saturated model, independent model, and those listed in Table 4.6. Recall that in entries listed as N (No), factor loadings β were constrained to 0, assuming these variables were unimportant in the model. They evaluated models on two levels. First, they checked their goodness of fit and examined possible reasons metrics could fluctuate. Second, they looked at significant factor loadings, namely significant *direct effects*, *indirect effects*, and *total effects*. This analysis led the authors to the following conclusions.

The best model for most metrics uses only background and experience measures – While not having the smallest χ^2 among the tested models, the BE model has the smallest χ^2/df. It also ranks the highest for adjusted AGFI, which adjusts GFI for parsimony, and obtains the lowest RMSEA score. It has a relatively low χ^2 and many degrees of freedom. This also helps to explain that while our full model has the best AIC score, the BE model has the lowest BIC score.

The best-fitting model uses all features, but it is not the simplest – While the full model performs best in χ^2 and unadjusted measures, it is one of the poorest performers in terms of adjusted measures. It has the worst AGFI and PGFI, and χ^2/df is on a par with the independent model assuming no relationships.

In general, intentions reduce χ^2 at the cost of goodness of fit – Keeping the background and experience constant, toggling the intents toggles the degrees of freedom by 20–40, with a small improvement in χ^2. Also, each model with intentions performs worse in several parsimony-based metrics with respect to its counterpart without intentions. This happens universally for χ^2/df, AGFI, PGFI, RMSEA, and BIC.

Experience variables account for much variance – All other factors held constant, removing the links to and from experience variables adds substantial χ^2. GFI, AGFI, and PGFI improve when removing experience, but most other metrics worsen.

None of the models is a particularly good fit–The saturated baseline can indeed be achieved by connecting all pairs of variables, and it perfectly fits the data. For good-fitting models, ideal fits for χ^2/df, GFI, AGFI, PGFI, and RMSEA are 2-5, 0.9, 0.9, 0.9, and 0.08, respectively. That said, the models are far from the ideal range, including the full model. This suggests that there are many connections not covered in this full model that should be included. This suggests potential gaps in the literature.

All of these led to the following conclusions.

Inasmuch as covered by this model, there are still direct paths from task type to browser signals – There are very frequently total and direct effects from task goal, product, and topic to the browser features. This may be a genuine direct effect or due to some unrecorded variable.

Topic familiarity also plays an important role – Each time topic familiarity was included in the model, it had a significant effect on the browsing features. Moreover, topic was only linked to topic familiarity and had significant indirect effects to certain browsing features 3–4 times, particularly query length, SERP dwell time, and number of pages. Therefore, topic influences these not only directly but indirectly through a user's topic familiarity.

Intentions can influence searchers' behavior, but influence from task type to intention was not found – Several direct effects from intentions to behaviors can were found. However, only task goal influences find/access/obtain intentions, even though it does so in every model. While intentions may influence their respective search session, perhaps intentions of a single query segment do not neatly map to task types. Perhaps intentions aggregated over an entire session map neatly to task type but not within a single query segment (counter to [12]). In the data, this would make a difference: even though there are 693 query segments and the same number of corresponding intention vectors, there are only 80 sessions on two task products, two task goals, and two topics.

There is some influence from a user's background – Occasionally, a user's search expertise and journalism expertise affects browsing behaviors, but are not affected by task.

We can see from this case study that not only is such a comprehensive model necessary, but our current understanding of how these variables relate to each other is perhaps incomplete. Specifically, we learned that task type seems to directly affect browsing, but this effect is some-what mediated by user factors like topic familiarity. We further learned there are other variables that—agreeing with previous literature—clearly affect browsing. The effectiveness of browsing behavior to predict task type will ultimately be affected by variance in things like task difficulty, time pressure, and intentions, which are difficult to control but should be accounted for. We expanded on previous literature with our complex path analysis yet still found several findings that agree with past work.

4.3 SUMMARY

Much of the literature in IR that deals with task is situated around the idea that the user either does not give us their task information or we cannot or should not ask them directly. And there-fore, these works attempt to infer task information from other signals. Sometimes it is already known (e.g., a student working on an assigned homework problem) or given. We explored the latter possibility with a case study where a user had explicitly expressed their tasks in a to-do application. While having the clear expression of task is quite advantageous, it is not always enough as we may lack other contextual factors. In the case study reported here, we explored a simple case of taking a task title and associating it with a search engine query. Of course, several tasks can be done using one or two queries, but more complex (and interesting) tasks require more than a query or question.

There are also times when we need to look at user behaviors and explicate task information. A significant challenge here is to figure out what specifically about the task do we want to extract. Do we treat task as a single, scalar variable? Or is it a multi-dimensional construct? There are studies that look at a task along an individual dimension of type (fact-finding, advise-seeking, exploration), complexity, or the support they need. There are also works that aim to extract multiple dimensions of a task. Often, the approach comes down to the "why" question—why are we interested in extracting task information? Is it to understand and explain what the user has done or is doing? Or is it to find an appropriate support that caters to that particular task? As we will see in the next chapter, this question becomes a critical one as we associate the task knowledge that we are explicating to the application or situation where we want to apply that knowledge.

CHAPTER 5

Applying Task Information for Search and Recommendations

We now come to a place where we have obtained task knowledge using some mechanism—either explicitly expressed by the user or explicated from other implicit signals—and we want to use it in enhancing search and recommendation applications. However, we want to do more than simply improve their performance; this chapter will show how we could even address the kind of problems we could not do without task knowledge. We will start with summarizing some of the existing research (and there is not that much) that directly apply task information to search or recommendation applications. Then we will look at a case study that uses reinforcement learning-based approach for incorporating task information in a ranking model.

5.1   FEW EXISTING EFFORTS

Existing research has used task information at various levels in IR-based applications. Some of the prominent ideas and outcomes in this space have demonstrated that task representations can be used to provide users with better query suggestions [14], offer improved personalization [216, 338], recommendation [372], and help in satisfaction prediction [110, 322].

Perhaps the more frequent and widespread use of task representations is to build user models for personalized search and recommendation settings (e.g., [216, 338]). Mehrotra et al. [214] used a tensor-based approach, representing each user as a combination of their topical interests and their search task behaviors for personalization. Other works have developed various novel task context embedding to learn the representation of queries by leveraging their task context information from historical search logs to provide task-based personalization, query suggestion, and re-ranking [216, 220]. Tolomei et al. [304] investigated the concept of task flows and analyzed a large-scale query log to generate task-based query suggestions. Baraglia et al. [21] introduced the notion of search shortcuts and offered query suggestions to drive users toward their goals.

Vu [320] has also used tasks to model user interests in search. In the similar vein but in other contexts, several scholars (e.g., [2, 137, 341]) have leveraged task information to provide long-term support for task completion. Cai et al. [55] used task models to improve the ranking of retrieved search results to provide task-based support to users. Tasks help users achieve their search goals and understand and evaluate a system's competency in helping users do so. Along this line, Hassan [110] used search task construct to predict users' satisfaction with the system, and White and Kelly [346] used it to improve users' relevance feedback. Song and Guo [290] also demonstrated that task information could be useful to automate a particular task in order to reduce user burden.

Other researchers have focused on assistive systems in terms of tours or trails to lead users through their search process [112, 238], predicting users' next search action in the immediate future based on the current actions, either by predicting the next result click [56] or by predicting users' short-term interests based on task topic information [336].

5.2   CASE STUDY: USING TASK INFORMATION FOR RECOMMENDATION APPLICATIONS

Now we will take a look at a very recent work by Sarkar and Shah that considers task context in which the user interacts with the system by sequentially selecting recommendation items over a sequence of time to maximize the cumulative reward. They define this problem as a Markov Decision Process (MDP), which includes a sequence of states, actions, and rewards as described below.

- **States (S):** the set of all states s_t which is a combination of users' implicit and explicit feedback at time t.

- **Actions (A):** the set of all actions a_t that synthesizes the ranked list from a finite set of available options, such as adding an item into the list, at time t during the search process.

- **Rewards (R):** the set of all rewards $r_a(s, s')$ represents the user's feedback on the recommended items after transition from state s to state s' with action a, which can be quantified by providing ratings or clicking or not clicking/rating.

- **Transition Probability (P):** the probability $P(s' \mid s, a)$ of state transitions from s to s' with action a.

Therefore, the problem statement of their framework is posed as: given the structural space of (S, A, P, R), can we offer a user the best recommendation policy $\pi : S \to A$ (i.e., a list of the relevant items), which will eventually maximize the cumulative reward for the search system?

To solve the MDP, an intuitive method is to calculate the optimal action-value functions $Q^*(s, a)$. The authors define the future cumulative reward at time t as $R_t = \sum_{t'=t}^{T} \gamma^{t'-t} r_{t'}$, where T is the time when the optimal ranked list is recommended, and γ is a discount factor. This gives $Q^*(s, a) = \max_\pi \mathbb{E}[R_t | s_t = s, a_t = a, \pi]$. Following the *Bellman equation*, the optimal action-value function can be calculated iteratively:

$$Q^*(s, a) = \mathbb{E}_{s' \sim S}\left[r + \gamma \cdot \max_{a'} Q^*(s', a') \mid s, a\right], \tag{5.1}$$

where $Q^*(s', a')$ is the optimal value at the next time step. However, due to the large size of both states S and actions A here, it is impractical to calculate the optimal action-value functions using Equation 5.1. Instead, the authors adopt Deep Q-learning Networks (DQN) to train a Q-network with weights θ to approximate $Q(s, a; \theta) \approx Q^*(s, a)$. The loss function of Q-network is defined as:

$$L_i(\theta_i) = \mathbb{E}_{s,a \sim \rho(.)} \left[(y_i - Q(s, a; \theta))^2 \right], \tag{5.2}$$

where $y_i = \mathbb{E}_{s' \sim S}[r + \gamma \cdot \max_{a'} Q^*(s', a'; \theta_{i-1}) \mid s, a]$ is the target for iteration i and $\rho(s, a)$ is a probability distribution over state s and actions a. When training the Q-network, they differentiate $L_i(\theta_i)$ with respect to weight θ, i.e., $\nabla_{\theta_i} L_i(\theta_i)$, to calculate the gradient.

5.2.1   THE PROPOSED FRAMEWORK

Typically, a task is conceptualized either as a multi-dimensional abstract construction or a concrete sequence of actions. Based on prior work, a task may be perceived as a notion independent of users and their search process. However, users may implicitly convey some individual traits with respect to the current task during the search process, such as their prior knowledge about the topics relevant to the task, and at the same time, may bring their own qualities independently of the task (e.g., their general search expertise). Therefore, the task context of an information retrieval and filtering process can be defined as a combination of task topic (what), search intention (why), and strategy (how). The framework proposed by the authors deconstructs the task contexts—*what, why,* and *how* in large-scale search logs by examining the associations between user behaviors (i.e., searching, browsing, and clicking) and task contexts to improve users' search experiences.

The framework is divided into these five phases.

- Phase 1: identify necessary user-system and user-item interaction data from past user studies and build *background, user,* and *activity* models using reverse modeling process.

- Phase 2: extract topic, intention, and strategy information using these models.

- Phase 3: build a reinforcement learning enhanced *learning-to-rank prediction model* which provides a list of ranked recommendations.

- Phase 4: validate the model's capability to predict the next activity and outcome in a search/browse session.

- Phase 5: evaluate the models with publicly available large web search logs.

The premise behind the framework is that if the system knows one's task, it is better for recommendation applications than just knowing user actions. The authors hypothesize, as it has been a central premise of this book, that we could provide better recommendations tailored toward their information need if we know someone's task.

5.2.2   PHASES 1 AND 2

To synthesize effective recommendations, a search system ideally requires three kinds of information: user's past behaviors, world knowledge, and user's current behavior [276]. Based on these three types of features, it is possible to create three predictive models: a *background model* (M_B), and *user model* (M_U), and an *activity model* (M_A), respectively, to describe the user's task context. M_U is associated with users' past actions for both short-term and long-term, such as queries formulated, SERPs viewed, pages/items clicked in previous search sessions at a given time, or multiple sessions in the past. Similarly, M_A, the activity model, is associated with user-item or user-query-item interactions at a given moment.

M_B, on the other hand, represents a task and user features dependent or independent of each other such as the overall goal of the task, users' knowledge, and perception about the task or topic.

Collectively, these three attributes from the short-term and long-term history of a user's search activity, along with other contextual task-user inherent characteristics, can model the user's past task topics and search strategies, and what and how they are trying to do now. Each model contains information for an action, its response, and an assessment of the resulting usefulness (e.g., whether the user clicked or bookmarked). The three predictive models could be represented as follows:

$$M_A = f_\alpha \left(\bigcup_i RS_i, \bigcup_i activity_i \right) \tag{5.3}$$

$$M_B = f_\beta \left(\bigcup_i RS_i, \bigcup_i activity_i \right) \tag{5.4}$$

$$M_U = f_\gamma \left(\bigcup_i RS_i, \bigcup_i activity_i \right), \tag{5.5}$$

where RS_i and $activity_i$ represent the result set and user activity associated with the i-th query segment, respectively. Moreover, f_α, f_β, and f_γ describe the relationship (potentially nonlinear) between relevant variables.

How much and what kind of behavioral data contribute to detecting the task context can be drawn from existing lab and field studies. While existing studies have identified various searching and browsing behaviors and facets and attributes of task and users, many existing search and recommendation system logs do not use all of them as they are not relevant or of no interest. For example, the MovieLens dataset does not contain click-through data. Amazon product review data also does not contain queries issued by the users to retrieve products (further details in the next section). Therefore, in the approach reported by the authors, they tried to extract implicit queries from the final search result accepted by the users and product relevance or experience feedback provided by the users at the end of their task using reverse modeling. Based on the relationships between the query, intent, and user response, they retroactively traced

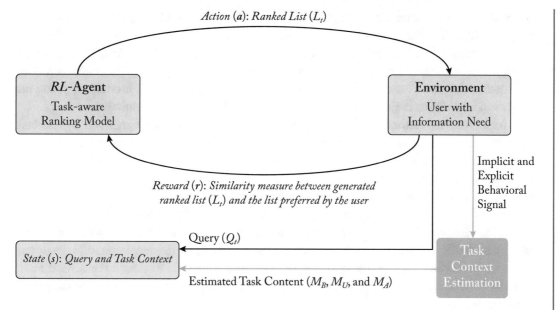

Figure 5.1: Overview of the task-aware reinforcement learning enhanced predictive model (taRLM). It highlights the interaction between a *task-aware ranking model* and a user with specific information need to accomplish a task.

back the user's search path to users' query or search intent from the search result they received and reviewed. Once they established the intent, they tried to infer the broader tasks, which motivated them to search for a particular product. To validate the synthetic task contexts, the authors applied their reverse models on previous user study data, which contained all the task-user features carefully collected from the users, and compared the synthetic data inferred from the reversed models with the labels provided by the users.

5.2.3   PHASE 3

To synthesize a ranked list of relevant items, the authors developed a task-aware reinforcement learning [298] enhanced predictive model *taRLM*. In reinforcement learning, an agent repeatedly interacts with its environment in order to learn an optimal policy, i.e., how to take actions in different situations, which subsequently maximizes the associated reward. For example, in the current context, the task-aware ranking model is the RL-*agent*, and the user, i.e., the information seeker, constitutes the *environment*. Figure 5.1 shows a schematic of the proposed predictive model. In what follows, the authors formulate the underlying MDP and describe how different aspects of the problem maps into the RL-framework. The reasons they decided to use a reinforcement learning-based framework: (1) reinforcement learning based model can continuously update strategies during user-system interactions; and (2) they can learn a strategy that maximizes the long-term cumulative reward from users.

The authors define the problem as an MDP with associated states, actions, and rewards to investigate how estimating task context from implicit behavioral signals can aid ranking models. In particular, they use a combination of the background model (M_B), user model (M_U), and user activity model (M_A) to define the underlying state (s_t) of the MDP formulation.

Moreover, the authors define the action a_t as the ranked list synthesized by the task-aware ranking model. As users' search queries within a single search session are focused on accomplishing a specific task, a recommended ranked list at a given time step will influence the search query and associated behavioral signals at the next time step. By treating this transition dynamics as a Markov process, this formulation assumes that the system state switches from its current value (s_t) to the future value (s_{t+1}) according to a transition probability $P(s_{t+1} \mid s_t, a_t)$. During the course of a specific search session, a user browses the recommended ranked list and provides feedback by clicking or bookmarking or not clicking on the recommended document. In this formulation, they use this information, i.e., user feedback, to define the reward as the similarity between the recommended ranked list and the list preferred by the user in the ground truth dataset.

The authors adopt Deep Q-learning to estimate the optimal action-value functions $Q^*(s, a)$, as shown in Algorithm 5.1, to solve the MDP. Specifically, they first initialize the experience replay memory capacity and the action-value function Q. Then they train the Q-network using the combination of ϵ-greedy policy, minibatch updates, and samples of experience to approximate $Q^*(s, a)$.

5.2.4   PHASES 4 AND 5

It is crucial to evaluate the effectiveness of the model and its components using criteria against a set of standards before implementing them. In general, the goal of the evaluation is the quality of the retrieved results as we will see in the next chapter. The specific study designs and effectiveness measures vary by domains and research problems. Depending on the nature of retrieved results, measurement of quality, various techniques of IR system evaluation is used. The test-collection approach can be used to measure the quality and efficiency of retrieved results using various metrics such as (MAP) [79], Discounted cumulative gain (DCG), and Normalized DCG (nDCG) [246]. Overall, these traditional measures allow a direct comparison of the baseline(s), the experimental condition, and the simulation runs.

5.2.5   DATASETS

In the reported experiments, the authors train their framework using five datasets—two in the context of movie and product search and recommendation and three session-based information retrieval datasets. All five of them are publicly available and widely used in search recommenda-

Algorithm 5.1 : Estimating $Q^*(s,a)$ using DQN

Initialize replay memory $\mathcal{D}$
Initialize action-value function Q with random weights

1: **for** $episode = 1 \rightarrow N$ **do**
2:      Initialize the start state s_1
3:      **for** $t = 1 \rightarrow T$ **do**
4:          With probability ϵ select a random action at a_t
5:          otherwise select $a_t = max_a Q^*(s_t, a; \theta)$
6:          Execute action a_t and calculate reward r_t and compose the next state s_{t+1}
7:          Store transition (s_t, a_t, r_t, s_{t+1}) in $\mathcal{D}$
8:          Sample random minibatch of transitions (s_j, a_j, r_j, s_{j+1}) from $\mathcal{D}$
9:          **if** s_{j+1} is terminal $y_j = r_j$ **then**
10:          **else** $y_j = r_j + \gamma max_{a'} Q(s_{j+1}, a'; \theta)$
11:          **end if**
12:          Perform a gradient descent step on $(y_j - Q(s_j, a_j; \theta))^2$ according to $\nabla_{\theta_i} L_i(\theta_i)$
13:      **end for**
14: **end for**

tions and retrieval studies. They used the TREC Session Track datasets to evaluate their model's retrieval performance.

Yandex   This dataset is a fully anonymized user session corpus from the Yandex search log shared as part of the Personalized Web Search Challenge.[1] Unlike the previous three, this dataset provides both long-term (one month of search history) and short-term (session history) contexts per user. The dataset contains 5,736,333 users, 21,073,569 unique queries, 703,484,26 unique item URLs, and 167,413,039 records in the log.

TREC Session Tracks 2013 and 2014   Session Tracks 2013 and 2014 from TREC[2] are comprised of search logs of users conducting searches over sessions, rather than performing ad-hoc retrieval. The 2014 dataset comprises 1,257 user sessions, with 260 unique users (from Amazon's Mechanical Turk) conducted searches across 60 different topics from four types of tasks (15 unique prompts per search task type). Session Track 2013 contains 442 queries and 87 sessions. The search tasks were designed based on two different combinations of task product and

---

[1]https://www.kaggle.com/c/yandex-personalized-web-search-challenge/overview
[2]https://trec.nist.gov/data/session.html

task goal (based on two task facets from [183]): (factual/amorphous) (intellectual/amorphous) (factual/specific) and (intellectual/specific).

From these three datasets, the following search behavioral features can be extracted: *query behavior*: number of queries, length of a query, query reformulation type; *browsing behavior*: number of clicks, the number of content pages visited; *dwell time (second)*: mean dwell time on each SERP, mean dwell time on each content page; total dwell time on content pages; and *usefulness judgment*: number of bookmarks, number of snippets. Based on these necessary measures, they further extracted three types of feature sets: (a) behavioral measures in the current query segment; (b) session-level behavioral measures prior to the current query segment; and (c) the combination of (a) and (b) sets.

MovieLens 20M Dataset   The authors used the 20M version of the MovieLens datasets.[3] This version contains 10 million user-item interactions with a minimum interaction of 20 per user. It is often used for evaluating CF models for movie recommendations. Since there is a single relevant item (one movie per query) per information need, there was not much variation in task types.

Amazon Product Review Datasets   The authors used another dataset in the context of e-commerce—the Amazon review dataset.[4] This large dataset contains user-item interactions on 24 product categories from May 1996 to July 2014. Among 24 categories, they extracted 2 different subsets of product categories—Kindle Store and Cell Phone—with different size and sparsity to observe the performance of the model on two different conditions. In these two categories, the minimum number of user-item interactions per user is 5.

5.2.6   EXPLICATING TASKS FROM AMAZON AND MOVIELENS DATASETS

The majority of real-life, large-scale, publicly available datasets do not contain any task information [366]. While Yandex and TREC datasets are complete datasets (e.g., have all contextual features or can be derived from existing features), MovieLens and Amazon do not have all the browsing features. For Yandex and TREC datasets, the authors used feature values accumulated from the start of a query segment (i.e., when the user first issued the query) until the next query (or for the last query, the end of the segment). Table 5.1 contains some examples of extracted queries and task descriptions.

To explicate task contexts from the MovieLens corpus, they used Stanford CoreNLP [208] to automatically generate potential queries that users could ask to get a movie name in answer. They first concatenated user-provided tags for each movie. We cleaned the tags and removed any non-alphabetic characters and non-English words/phrases.

---

[3]https://grouplens.org/datasets/movielens/20m/
[4]https://nijianmo.github.io/amazon/index.html#samples

Table 5.1: Example queries extracted from our reverse model

Example Queries Extracted Through Datasets Without Query

MovieLens:
  – Which movie based on a comic superhero chris evans
    hugo weaving marvel world war ii
  – What movie is based on a true story dogs loyalty

Amazon Kindle Store:
  – Amy Brewster Mystery
  – story about Chewbaccas son Lumpy

Amazon Cell Phone:
  – smartphone with large screen
  – phone with external storage

The review dataset does not contain query information. However, directed product search queries typically contain brand names, manufacturers' names, or other information describing the product category [257]. Therefore, based on this observation, Van Gysel et al. [314] proposed a query generation process to automatically generate queries based on the product categories. For example, for each item in a product category p, a query q is being generated based on the descriptive terms in the category hierarchy of p, and all the items within that category are marked as relevant for the query q. Although the queries were automatically constructed, it is a standard approach within the research community to generate queries from real-world data (e.g., [366, 370]).

For the Amazon datasets, the authors selected the most detailed and helpful review of each item based on users' helpfulness scores as the task description [366]. If there is no helpful score for an item review, they picked a review randomly. Then the authors cleaned up the data by removing special, non-ASCII characters and stop words. Furthermore, they evaluated the task extraction model trained on the Amazon datasets by using an automatic evaluation methodology [5, 313].

5.2.7   EXPERIMENTS WITH THE FRAMEWORK

Let us now look at the parameter training procedures. In this work, the authors utilized the DQN algorithm [229, 298] to train the parameters of the proposed framework. DQN is a model-free off-policy actor-critic algorithm, combining Q-Learning with deep neural networks. In DQN, when given a pair of state and action, the environment is supposed to return the reward. However, in this problem, one cannot observe real-time user response. Therefore, the authors used the existing data to judge the relevance of documents.

Table 5.2: Accuracy of methods: comparisons among various ranking models for TREC Session Track datasets

Model	TREC 2013 nDCG@10	TREC 2014 nDCG@10
TREC best	0.1952	0.2099
TREC median	0.1521	0.1170
Multi-MDP(MAX_QT)	0.2556	0.2107
Win-Win	0.2026	NA
taRLM	**0.2793**	**0.2373**

The authors trained and evaluated their task-aware ranking model with 70% training and 30% testing data. For each dataset, they used the first 70% of the search and recommendation sessions in temporal order as the training set and the later 30% sessions as the testing set. For a given session, the initial state was collected from the previous sessions of the user. They leveraged $N = 10$ previously clicked/reviewed/rated items as a positive state. Each time the model recommended a list of $K = 10$ items to users. The reward r of skipped/clicked/reviewed/rated items was empirically set as 0 and 1, respectively. For the parameters of the proposed framework, such as K and γ, they selected them via cross-validation. Correspondingly, they also did parameter-tuning for baselines for a fair comparison.

5.2.8   EVALUATION AND DISCUSSION

The authors conducted extensive experiments to evaluate the effectiveness of the proposed framework. They examined (1) how the proposed framework performs compared to representative baselines; and (2) how the task features contribute to the performance of the proposed framework. To evaluate the performance of their framework, they selected normalized discounted cumulative gain (nDCG) of the top 10 items (nDCG@10) as the metrics to measure the performance. nDCG is a ranking metric that accounts for the hit's position by assigning higher scores to hits at top ranks. For the TREC datasets with sessions data, they compared their model with TREC *best* and *median* [61] baselines. The authors compared with two additional learning-to-rank models: Win-Win [206] and Multi-MDP [68]. Both of them implemented the MDP-based learning models using TREC Session Track data to develop adaptive ranking models. Table 5.2 shows that their framework (significantly) outperformed all baseline models.

The authors compared taRLM's performance with five representative baselines:

- DQN: A Deep Q-network (without task features) [373].

- DNN: A deep neural network with back propagation technique.

Table 5.3: Accuracy of methods: comparisons among various recommendation models

Model	ML 20M nDCG	Amazon nDCG	Yandex nDCG	TREC 2013 nDCG	TREC 2014 nDCG
DQN	0.65	**0.78**	0.63	0.78	0.79
DNN	0.60	0.60	0.64	0.55	0.67
NCF	0.44	0.71	0.59	0.87	0.65
CDL	0.63	0.75	0.64	0.55	0.76
JSR	0.63	**0.78**	0.62	0.56	0.77
taRLM	**0.71**	0.77	**0.76**	**0.88**	**0.80**

- Neural Collaborative Filtering (NCF) [116]: a combination of a generalized matrix factorization and a fully-connected network.

- Collaborative Deep Learning (CDL) [324]: a neural network based hybrid-recommendation model.

- Joint Search and Recommendation model (JSR) [366]: a matrix factorization-based joint search and recommendation model.

The authors calculated both metrics for each test session and reported the average score across all sessions. Table 5.3 shows that for MovieLens and Amazon Review datasets, their framework achieves comparable performance with DQN, CDL, and JSR. This result indicates that taRLM is suitable for adaptive search systems and works for ad-hoc/non-session data. For session-based complete datasets, i.e., the data from the Yandex and TREC Session tracks, taRLM outperforms other baselines significantly. To sum up, according to the Table 5.3, the proposed model produced a somewhat comparable performance using task-context information. It performed significantly better than the most representative baselines. To validate their framework's effectiveness, they investigated how the proposed framework taRLM performs with task features changes while fixing other parameters. They ran their model on the TREC 2014 Session track, both with the task aspects and without them. The results showed that the proposed framework can indeed boost ranking performance with task features. All of these findings, once again, demonstrate the importance of task aspects in the search system context.

5.3   SUMMARY

The research literature is filled with studies over the last several decades that try to understand and explain the task one has as they work through an information seeking episode. Often the motivation for doing so is to determine appropriate support that we could provide to that user for that situation. As it has been a core premise of this book, addressing one's task rather than their individual query or question at a time could have far reaching implications for not only existing IR systems, but also emerging modalities that intelligent agents can support. However, when it comes to taking task information to doing just that, we do not find a flurry of existing works. It could be that we needed all this time, development of methodologies, and strong enough results about explicating task information before we could start using it reliably in IR applications. If that is the case, perhaps now we will start seeing more work that starts going beyond understanding and explicating task information, and incorporating that information in existing and new IR situations.

In this chapter, we described one such case study that attempted to incorporate task knowledge in a ranking application using a reinforcement learning approach. This case may appear to be a specific scenario with promising results, but the important point to take away from it is that there are systematic ways to consider task information in current methods of ranking (think search) and filtering (think recommendation). As this case study did, there are other current works and there will be more works that take a very specific, narrow approach to applying task information in an IR application. Perhaps that is all we need—application or situation specific application of task information. Or perhaps we can think about having a general-purpose representation of task that is independent of applications or situations. We will revisit this idea in the last chapter as we talk about future directions.

CHAPTER 6

Task-Based Evaluation

Evaluation is a critical topic in search and recommendation [146]. System designers need to understand, based on offline studies and experiments with human subjects, what works well and what needs improvement. When it comes to task-based search and recommendation, we must consider how well systems support aspects of the task completion process and the attainment of task outcomes. The task completion process is often complex and exists within situations that extend well beyond the engagement with information systems (e.g., elsewhere in the task life cycle (e.g., preparation, use) [130] and more broadly, considering associated contexts [126]). It is insufficient to evaluate task support based solely on specific aspects of the system (e.g., click-through rates on lists of recommended items). We need to evaluate complex systems both holistically and per component to reach actionable conclusions and understand how well these systems are doing. There are many choices for methodologies and metrics, and it is not always apparent which ones to use. In this chapter, we will cover several such metrics and show, through several case studies, how they can be used and what they can tell us about the capabilities of systems being designed to provide task support to users.

Given the interactive nature of the systems we describe, there is an important human element in the evaluation process; it is insufficient to solely target system functionality when systems and people must work together synergistically to complete tasks [24]. This is already an active research area. For example, Järvelin et al. [130] proposed a theoretical framework for task-based information interaction (TBII) evaluation derived from program theory [255]. The TBII evaluation framework considers systems within, albeit limited, contexts, and cognitive states that evolve over the course of the task. It studies system contributions toward task outcomes, where the system includes the role of the human actor. Despite their promise, it is challenging to build these frameworks without supporting data. The TBII framework focuses on general level models, specific (learning-based) tasks, and ignores the social/collaborative aspects that underlie many tasks [273, 275].

In this chapter, although we cover evaluation methodologies briefly at the outset (primarily for completeness), we mainly focus on evaluation *metrics*. These are the measures used to compute task performance and focusing on them enables us to explicate the various ways that systems can support task accomplishment and avoid being too narrowly focused on specific systems or components. The key questions we answer in this chapter include: (i) How do we measure system performance in task-based settings? (ii) How do we determine task progress and task completion? (iii) How do we assess the performance of systems supporting proactive experiences designed to boost awareness and task completion?

Before diving into the details, let us begin with an example. Imagine a system that supports complex tasks via voice interactions. We will discuss such a system in more detail in one of the case studies in Section 6.5. That system could have an automatic speech recognizer (evaluated using a metric such as word error rate), an intent understanding model (or models) (with a metric such as accuracy), question answering component (with a metric such as answer correctness), and so on. The performance of those individual elements is certainly important, but it is the performance of the full system (all components combined) that matters most to users and will determine the quality of the user experience. We need integrated metrics [306] and we need to consider how the components interact, compounding errors in chained components (e.g., a speech recognition error may cause an intent understanding error), and other issues (such as how to interpret integrated metrics when the underlying user or task model may be unclear). All of these elements contribute to task success, one *holistic* measure of system effectiveness. We will describe a range of holistic metrics, and also discuss combining them and factors that affect them. We conclude with case studies illustrating the application of these metrics in practice.

6.1   METHODOLOGIES

There are many standard practices in evaluation methods (user study protocols, instruments, etc.) that apply to evaluating task-based systems (see [146] for an excellent summary). These methods can be offline, without live users and focused on specific components of a system (e.g., ranking effectiveness) in highly controlled settings, or online, with less control but more realism. In information retrieval (IR), the Cranfield experiments [73] and TREC [318] have been essential in driving progress in the development of benchmark test collections and new ranking algorithms. TREC even featured a Tasks Track from 2015–2017 (see [362] for more details). Cranfield and TREC abstract away many of the human elements and focus on top resources and the document to query match. Beyond Cranfield and TREC, evaluation of search and recommendation systems is now taking a broader view on tasks, users, and context [136], helping to improve the realism of the experiments and the reliability of the conclusions drawn from them.

Alternative methods include laboratory studies (using simulated work tasks [44]), retrospective log analysis (which offers a limited lens on tasks, i.e., only what is observable through user actions), A/B testing (which is being used extensively by major search providers [162] (absolute performance) alongside interleaving [63] (relative performance)), ethnographic (small-scale observation-based) studies [89], and simulations of search behavior [316, 344] (which must be validated prior to use [242]). Evaluating intelligent systems in situ [88] considers the realities of how people use systems in practice (e.g., diverse sets of users/tasks/intents; natural interaction) versus the static benchmark test collections used extensively in IR evaluation [264].

Tasks often extend over time and can be part of larger macrotasks (e.g., planning a wedding, taking a vacation). Longitudinal studies are time consuming to perform and experimenters must sacrifice some control, which is good for realism but can lessen the generalizability of the claims that can be made from the findings. Methods such as "living laboratories" [152] can help bridge user-centered research and system-centered research, enabling comparative evaluation over systems and time. They include resources, tools, and infrastructure for collaborative experimentation. Efforts to date have focused living laboratories on specific settings, e.g., popular queries [19] or cross-language [271]. Combinations of methods (so-called "mixed methods" studies) provide a more complete picture than that available from a single method (e.g., retrospective analysis of search engine query logs [105]), coming at the cost of additional study complexity and resource expenditure.

6.2   METRICS

As mentioned earlier, despite the broad array of methodologies, the focus of this chapter is on task-based evaluation metrics. Metrics are central to understanding how systems are performing and where they can improve. Evaluating systems on the basis of task performance (e.g., the extent to which users were able to solve problems using search) has been explored for decades [117]. Search and recommendation systems are only a means to an end, a tool to support some aspects of task completion. To perform task-based evaluation, we need to consider both process metrics and outcome metrics. There may also be pre-task metrics, associated with preparation and preparedness, but those are more user- and scenario-dependent than system dependent (so we will not focus on those in this chapter). All metrics make (often implicitly) assumptions about user behavior when performing a task. Conceptualizing tasks and creating task models are important in determining appropriate evaluation metrics. These models must be validated against real user behavior in log data [92].

We group these holistic metrics into two categories: process and outcome.[1] The metrics space is incredibly rich and we will not have an opportunity to discuss all metrics from each category in this chapter. We aim to highlight a few important metrics that are especially relevant to task-based scenarios and mostly measurable at scale, and provide some pointers for the reader to learn more about the other metrics as desired.

Process
Process metrics are focused on how people attempt to complete the task, regardless of the task outcome. The primary metrics we will cover in depth are:

- **Time:** The time taken to complete the task; both the actual time and the time as perceived (which can differ from stopwatch time, e.g., during flow [82]).

---

[1]Later in the chapter, especially when we get to the case studies, we will also break out metrics by holistic (about overall task performance) and per component (about a specific system element). Per these definitions, all of the metrics we focus on in Section 6.2 are "holistic" and applicable across systems and scenarios.

- **Effort:** The user effort expended to complete the task (e.g., the number of actions, such as queries issued, recommendations reviewed, or dialog turns).

- **Engagement:** The connection between the user and the system, spanning emotional, cognitive, and behavioral aspects.

- **Progress:** How far through the task the user has gotten, including simply whether or not the task is yet completed (binary signal, independent of success), or more detailed task status (e.g., 80% complete).

These four popular metrics are broadly applicable across tasks and systems, are easy to define, and can mostly be computed at low cost and at large scale. We elect to leave out metrics such as the following.

- **Cognitive load:** The demands placed on people's cognitive capacities by the task and/or the system (e.g., [60]). This has been studied in search and recommendation, e.g., in search, both Beaulieu [25] and Bruza et al. [48] examined cognitive load in the context of query reformulation.

- **Learning:** The amount of new knowledge gained or the cognitive transformation that has occurred during the task completion process (e.g., [3]). This has been well explored in task-based search and recommendation, e.g., Eickhoff et al. [93] studied within- and cross-session learning during searching, Liu et al. [190] studied knowledge change during task completion, and Rieh et al. [252] examined search as a learning process.

- **Affect:** The impact on user emotional state of performing the task on the system, e.g., Feild et al. [97] analyzed user frustration during the search process.

- **Usability:** The ability to perform tasks while also enjoying the experience (e.g., [7]). Usability is a complex construct that is closely connected to the user experience and may include some of the metrics that we focus on here (e.g., efficiency, effectiveness, and satisfaction [100]).

Many of the excluded process metrics are more abstract and more challenging to define and measure, especially at large scale in operational systems (proxies are not easy to define). Nonetheless, they are still important and need to be understood as part of developing a comprehensive picture of task effectiveness.

Outcome

Outcome metrics are focused on the product of the tasks, either a real outcome (e.g., achieving task completion, obtaining relevant information) or a user-perceived outcome (like satisfaction). We focus on the following three outcome metrics.

- **Utility:** The value of information obtained to complete the task, with a special focus on relevance, a core construct in search, and recommendation.

- **Success:** Whether the task objective was accomplished. This need not be binary; users can be partially successful at accomplishing tasks.

- **Satisfaction:** Whether users were happy with the outcome of the task and the process. This may be a function of the task completion process, as well as a successful task outcome.

The data required to calculate these metrics can be collected directly from users (e.g., via in-situ surveys [98]) or inferred from user activity. There are many other metrics that we will not have an opportunity to cover in this chapter, including the following.

- **Novelty and diversity:** The amount of new and/or diverse information obtained during the task, e.g., surfaced by a search engine [71].

- **Creativity:** New task-relevant thoughts and ideas that come from using the system and performing the task, e.g., in creativity support tools [284].

- **Adoption and retention:** The long-term impact of using the task system, including whether users return to that system for the same or similar tasks over time, e.g., in search engine switching [345] and sustained use [89].

Once again, the excluded metrics are less well defined and depend on access to data that may not be available (e.g., creativity is challenging to measure, novelty is difficult to determine, retention requires tracking user activity over time in ways that may not even be permissible given privacy considerations).

Additional Considerations

Beyond the metrics listed above, there are many others that are important in evaluating search and recommendation systems, including robustness, privacy, adaptivity, and scalability [281]. In developing and applying these metrics, we also need to consider user models (personas, experienced searchers with clearly defined tasks, e.g., a librarian or other search intermediary) and task models (a variety of different search strategies and goals [23, 363]). It is also important to understand the nature of the user experience. For example, search and recommendation systems might have quite different engagement models (search is usually reactive, while recommendation is usually proactive). This will impact how the metrics are defined and interpreted, e.g., it might be appropriate to track interruptions and suggestion acceptance as part of evaluating a recommendation system but likely not a search system. Also, metrics do not exist in isolation—they interact with one another, e.g., effort affects satisfaction [361] and they trade off, e.g., time taken versus coverage [306]. As such, metrics need to be contextualized, e.g., not all effort is detrimental (extra time and effort to get the same result), however, more effort could also mean

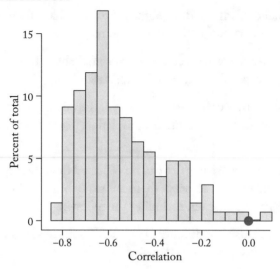

Figure 6.1: Histogram of correlations between task completion times and satisfaction for each user. Note the strongly negative correlation of task completion time and user satisfaction. The results suggest that the shorter the total time on task, the more likely users are to be satisfied. The red dot signifies no correlation. Figure adapted from [357].

learning more about different perspectives, enabling a user to be more informed and make better decisions.

6.2.1 TIME

The final process metric we focus on is time on task. Time on task has been used extensively as a productivity and usability metric [84]. In search systems, task completion time has been used for search evaluation [357]. Xu and Mease [357] showed that time on task is negatively correlated with user satisfaction: lower time to task completion means more user satisfaction. Figure 6.1 shows the histogram of per-user time-satisfaction correlations from their study.

The time spent on specific documents has been used as a satisfaction signal, e.g., so-called "decision time" (the time taken to decide whether a document is useful or not) [191] or "dwell time" [98]. Task has been shown to affect times [150] and they can vary per task, per individual, and both combined [346].

Expanding to full sessions, Smucker and Clarke [288] studied time from the perspective of gain per unit time (so-called "time-based gain" (TBG)), moving past some of the simplifying assumptions about user behavior in current effectiveness measures (some of which we will discuss in Section 6.2.5). As we try to model tasks in a search context, we often find ourselves discussing *sessions* (sequences of interactions demarcated by topic or time [137]), which are not exactly the

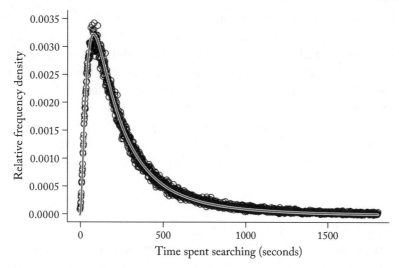

Figure 6.2: Empirical distribution of time spent searching (from first search to last click). Each circle is the fraction of the user population searching for that time. There is clear variability in search time across the population. Figure adapted from [72].

same as tasks (especially given multi-tasking [293]) but are a reasonable proxy for task in a search setting and could also be a source of more direct data on tasks [185].

In [288], the authors consider the fact that rather than spending an equal amount of time per document, as is often assumed, users in fact spend much longer on some documents than others. The plot in Figure 6.2 shows the amount of variation in total search times for a task (time from first search to last click) in one of their studies on this topic, based on search log data [72]. The time required to complete the performed task is influenced by aspects such as document length, duplicates, and summaries. TBG explicitly accommodates such aspects of the search process in an evaluation metric that enables search systems to be compared.

Human factors researchers have developed GOMS, a human information processor model for HCI observation that describes a user's cognitive structure in four components: goals, operators, methods, and selections [60]. GOMS is a widely used method by usability specialists, offering quantitative and qualitative predictions of how people will use a proposed system. With GOMS, an analyst can easily estimate a particular interaction and calculate it quickly and easily. This is only possible if the average "methods-time measurement" (MTM) [211] data for each specific task has been accurately measured experimentally [135]. MTM is a predetermined motion time system that is used primarily in industrial settings to analyze the methods used to perform any manual operation or task and set the standard time in which a worker should complete that task.

Moving beyond search and beyond objective (stopwatch based) assessments of time can be challenging for many reasons. Subjective perceptions of elapsed time are subject to the effects of attentional demand (degree of focus on the task at hand) [82, 365], experience with the task [303], and task difficulty (e.g., for easy tasks, people tend to overestimate time [43]). Similarly, people can face challenges in forecasting the amount of time a task will take. They have a tendency to underestimate that time because of biases such as the "planning fallacy" (overconfidence) [140]. In recent work, we have used large-scale data and deep learning models to estimate the amount of time tasks will take [341], including detecting extremely short tasks (microtasks) [347], addressing some of the limitations of subjective time assessment.

6.2.2   EFFORT

Effort can be measured objectively as quantifiable measures of work involved in completing a task, or as effort perceived by the actors in task completion. Effort can assume many forms, depending on the application. In search, effort is typically connected to the number of searches or clicks that are needed (e.g., Azzopardi et al. [15] showed that query "cost" affects search behavior). In digital assistance, effort can be the number of actions or steps the user must take. In conversational experiences, it could be the number of dialog turns, including the number of clarifications, which may require additional effort. In recommendation systems, it might be the number of system suggestions the user needs to triage. Kelly [147] discussed the relationship between expected and experienced effort. She argued that if the experienced effort is less than expected, the task is considered easy; if experienced is similar to expected, the task is considered moderately difficult, and; if the experienced effort is more than expected, the task is considered difficult.

Effort underlies many of the user models in IR evaluation. Effort-based models fix a certain effort and measure the utility in terms of relevance retrieved. Examples of associated metrics, DCG and nDCG [129], and other rank-based metrics (e.g., graded average precision (GAP) [253], rank biased precision (RBP) [232], and expected reciprocal rank (ERR) [64]), all assume searcher effort is linear to the (expected) number of examined results [131]. Utility-based models fix a certain utility and measure the effort needed to obtain it. Examples of associated metrics are mean average precision (MAP) and other recall-based metrics. Dupret and Piwowarski [92] argued that predicting user behavior in search sessions requires user models (developed based on intuition- and/or data-derived assumptions about how people will engage) that neither fix effort and utility, but combine both in a single model. In doing so, they unlocked a new line of research incorporating the dynamic, interactive aspects of information seeking behavior. Dupret and Piwowarski's focus on comparing user models rather than metrics is useful, since user model fidelity can be established independently [142].

Research on information foraging theory (IFT) considers the amount of gain obtained as a function of the time/effort invested in a particular path [244]. IFT has its roots in marginal value theorem (MVT) [65]. MVT is an optimality model describing the behavior of an optimally

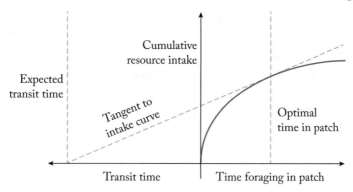

Figure 6.3: Visual depiction of marginal value theorem. Resource intake (solid curved line on right) increases but plateaus as resources are depleted. Transit time ends when a new patch is encountered. The tangent to the intake curve maximizes the ratio between resource intake and time spent foraging and traveling.

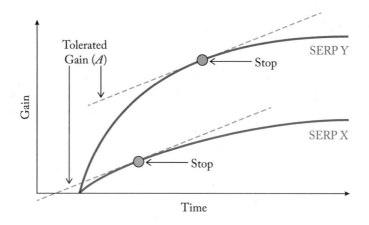

Figure 6.4: Visual depiction of the MVT applied to search, with two different SERPs (X and Y) with different gain curves. Searchers will likely abandon the SERP when the gain drops below the tolerated gain A. Figure adapted from [16].

foraging individual in a system where resources are located in discrete patches separated by regions with no resources (necessitating inter-patch transit time). See Figure 6.3 for a visual depiction of the MVT.

Researchers have applied IFT and similar concepts in the context of search [16, 231], considering the amount of gain searchers obtain as they navigate search engine result pages (SERPs). Azzopardi et al. [16] argued that searchers will stop examining a SERP when the rate of gain falls below the tolerated gain (*A* in Figure 6.4). At that point, the searcher will likely reformulate their query or stop searching.

IR researchers have long considered effort to be a core part of the search process. Cooper [78] proposed a metric called "expected search length" (ESL), based on the expected number of documents that had to be read to encounter relevant content. Dunlop [91] extended the ESL metric to measure the expected time required to find a certain amount of relevant results. Kazai et al. [144] proposed "effort-precision," the ratio of effort (number of examined results) to find the same amount of relevant information in the ranked list compared with an ideal list. These methods all assume that examining different results involves the same effort. Research on TBG (discussed earlier) [288] and the "U-measure" [262] (similar in some respects to TBG, but flexible enough to also handle other SERP elements, e.g., snippets, direct answers) have gone some way to addressing this. Beyond search, recent work in the context of intelligent assistance has shown that user satisfaction is negatively correlated with the amount of effort to complete the task: more effort means less user satisfaction [160].

6.2.3   ENGAGEMENT

Engagement can be defined as "a user's response to an interaction that gains, maintains, and encourages their attention, particularly when they are intrinsically motivated" [127]. The intrinsic motivation aspect is important and describes the requirement that the interaction be driven by internal rewards, i.e., is satisfying to the user. Engagement covers the emotional, cognitive, and behavioral connection that exists at any point in time and over time, between users and the system [332]. Research in this area leverages a range of signals, from user activity (clicks, hovers, swipes, etc.) to self-reports and cognitive measures (physiological, perceptual).

The signals can be combined (e.g., think alouds plus user activity) to gain a more complete picture of user engagement, but in doing so experimenters must be cautious of interaction effects. For example, asking users to think aloud (express their thoughts as they try to complete the task) may interfere with passive monitoring of their activity. In addition, engagement can be affected by many factors, including user and task characteristics, the user experience, and various biases. O'Brien and Toms [170] and Lalmas et al. [237] both offer excellent summaries of research in this area.

It is worth noting that while engagement is important, it may not always be a central goal of task-based systems. In open-domain dialog systems, the primary goal is to maximize user engagement [122]. In contrast, task-oriented dialog systems focus on accomplishing a specific task in one or more domains [67].

6.2.4   PROGRESS

The final process metric we will consider is task progress. This describes how far through a task a user has gotten, or conversely, how close they are to completion. It also includes simply a binary determination of whether they have completed the task versus whether the task is still in

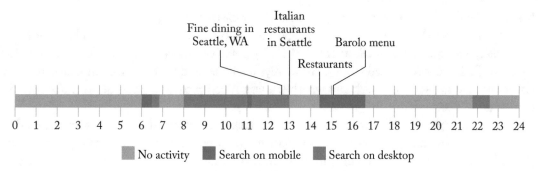

Figure 6.5: Cross-device timeline illustrating a task (find a local restaurant) spanning both mobile and desktop devices. This illustrates the complexity of real-world tasks and the need to support them across time and space. Figure adapted from [328].

progress. For the purposes of our discussion, we will decouple progress from success, an outcome measure that we will cover later. In analyzing task progress, we need to consider that tasks can be self-contained (simple, atomic tasks performed within a single session) or, as Figure 6.5 suggests, they can span multiple sessions [165] and multiple devices [233, 328] (complex, multi-faceted tasks with multiple dimensions requiring different resources), which can complicate the monitoring of task progress given the presence of many latent variables.

For some tasks, such as transactional tasks or fact-finding in online environments, where activities may be discernible and the answer may be known, detecting task completion may be straightforward, e.g., measure whether people reach the destination resource [337]. For other task types, such as learning tasks, we need to understand whether users obtain value from the journey itself [343], which can be more important in the long-term (e.g., in terms of cognitive development) than reaching a single destination. The user's mental model of the task becomes clearer as the task proceeds [311]. Related are studies of "flow" [82], a state of concentration so focused that it amounts to absolute absorption in an activity. Studies have shown that these optimal experiences occur when the task is clear and doable, we can concentrate sufficiently to become immersed in the task, we have control over progress, and get immediate feedback on progress. This is related to our earlier discussion of time (in Section 6.2.1); when users are in the flow, the sense of duration of time is altered (perceived time is shorter).

For many tasks, especially those in the physical world, we may only observe some user actions, making it difficult, if not impossible, to reliably track progress. Task progress can be tracked using dedicated tools [35] such as task management applications and project management systems. These can help track progress in individuals (offering reminders and a "mark complete" affordance) or teams (tracking dependencies, overall project completion percentage).

In practice, users may not explicitly mark tasks as complete, in which case, recent developments in automatic task completion detection can be useful [342]. Research has built benchmarks for measuring task progress in digital assistants [188] using the experience sampling method (ESM) [174] to collect task labels in situ (periodical and on-demand surveys) and using daily reconstruction method (DRM) [139] (recollect and label a sample of their tasks, e.g., [153]). The data collected from these surveys could be used to train machine-learned models to estimate the stage in a task and whether a task is complete at a given time and/or specific context(s).

In task-oriented dialog systems, where the task is clear and the information required is known (e.g., restaurant reservations), the focus tends to be on metrics such as the number of slots filled (x of y) [49]. Of course, that depends on knowledge of the task (total number of steps) and being able to observe the aspects of the task as it is performed, including the steps users have taken and the (sub-)task completion event(s). This is possible for stepwise tasks, such as cooking, reservations, and so on.

6.2.5   UTILITY

We now turn our attention to the first of the outcome metrics: utility. Belkin et al. [34] provide a methodological view to the problem of evaluating interactive IR. The main idea is centered on breaking down the information seeking episode into a sequence of interactions, each with a sequence of information seeking strategies, and propose to evaluate each interaction as well as the overall episode in term of metrics such as task accomplishment and perceived usefulness (defined with respect to the documents accessed, the result ranking itself, query suggestions presented, etc.).

In search and recommendation settings, the primary measure of utility is relevance. Relevance describes the value of the information encountered—irrespective of how it is encountered—in the course of attempting the task at hand. It is personal and situational [228]. Even within the same search task, relevance is affected by the stage in the task [302]. Relevance metrics (often based on topical match via third-party judgments) help estimate support for task completion (a proxy for task success). Many relevance metrics have been proposed, e.g., MAP, (n)DCG, RBP, precision at rank k (P@k), etc., all of which encode different user models [231]. These metrics are commonly used in search and recommendation evaluation to estimate system support for task completion. Multiple metrics can be used since they provide complementary information; the challenge is performing meta-analysis across multiple metrics and interpreting those metrics if they disagree. We can also use discriminative power to select the metric(s) best able to distinguish two differently performing systems [260].

Relevance metrics are usually computed per query. Session-level metrics such has the "cube test" [205] and session DCG [129] have also been proposed. As mentioned earlier, TREC ran a Tasks Track from 2015–2017, where the relevance of the results obtained was measured alongside utility for the task at hand and a separate task understanding challenge. Other TREC tracks are also relevant, namely the Session Track (focused on retrieval over multi-query sessions) [61] and Dynamic Domain Track (supporting dynamic and iterative search based on user feedback) [359].

One challenge with focusing on relevance for tasks is that while it reflects the potential value of the information encountered, it does not reflect task completion. Search results are often only the beginning of a task, especially for complex tasks. There are tasks that can be completed on search engines directly (e.g., those with instant answers; stock quotes, weather, etc.), but most require post-SERP activity and often activity in the physical world that may be unobservable to search providers. Focusing on post-SERP trails [185, 286] and destination pages mined from browsing logs is one way to define utility beyond the SERP [87, 337].

The practice of evaluating performance using benchmark assessments based on objective, topical relevance is also no longer sufficient. Such assessments do not generalize across searchers, and it is difficult to create benchmark judgments based on other types of relevance because they are even more individualistic by nature. Assessments are also dynamic [152]. Other types of relevance—situational, cognitive, and motivational [265]—will become increasingly important in the evaluation of task-based search and recommendation systems. Recent research on contextual search uses relevance judgments mined from individual behavior in search logs [38, 39].

Task-based search systems [220, 338], task-based recommendation systems [372], and session-based recommendation systems [118, 178] all mine and use on-task activity to identify items. The results and recommendations are often evaluated using standard retrieval metrics such as recall (fraction of relevant items retrieved), mean reciprocal rank, and nDCG, although other metrics such as scalability, stability (as new data arrives), and human preferences have also been used [204].

6.2.6 SUCCESS

Success is a measure of goal completion. It is related to satisfaction but not entirely. It is possible to be successful while also being dissatisfied with the task completion process. Success can be objective (whether or not the task outcome is factually correct or partially correct for multi-faceted outcomes) or subjective (is the task outcome perceived correct). The typical focus is on objective success, primarily because it usually matters more than a (possibly) unfounded belief and subjective success can also be biased.

In search engine evaluation, machine-learned models of task success trained based on user behavior (sequences of queries and clicks, with corresponding dwell times) have been shown to be more predictive than traditional measures such as DCG [109]. In recommendation settings, success can include acceptance of recommendations made and/or some follow-on action, e.g., a conversion to purchasing a recommended item [47]. As people try to complete tasks, they may experience some challenges in finding the information they need. Struggling is common during search tasks. Researchers have studied this, including distinguishing struggling from exploring in search sessions [114], and identifying pivotal queries in search tasks, after which more successful outcomes are observed despite initial difficulties [240].

Beyond search and recommendation, task success is often tied to end-to-end task completion: being able to place an order or make a reservation. This might be the case in search too (the so-called "last mile" in search interaction [333]) but the completion events can involve in-world activities that are unobservable to search engines. In more open-ended dialog (those supporting chit-chat, for example) success is often based on the system's ability to drive engagement and maintain a human-like conversation [189].

6.2.7   SATISFACTION

The last outcome metric that we will cover is satisfaction. Satisfaction is an emotional response that is more general than search success. It has been studied extensively in many communities, including psychology [199] and commerce [241].

In search, satisfaction modeling is mostly performed at the task/session level [111]. Research in this area led to the popular 30-second dwell time threshold for satisfied clicks [98]. If users view a landing page for more than that time, they are assumed to be satisfied. Although attractive, this is an oversimplification. Satisfaction is non-binary and there are clearly many factors that can contribute. These include task and user effects [150, 346] (including topic and task complexity [157]), which have been shown to affect many aspects of dwell time. Research into query level, graded, and personalized satisfaction modeling has also been performed [113, 133].

Result relevance has been shown to be a strong predictor of session satisfaction [123]. Where the satisfaction occurs within the task or session is important. The last query has more impact [132]: nDCG of last query is more correlated with overall satisfaction (also see [197, 198]). Attempts have been made to incorporate recency effects to construct more robust task/session-level evaluation metrics [368].

Even more sophisticated behavioral analysis, now factoring in touch and voice interactions, have been used to model user satisfaction on intelligent assistants, yielding reasonable accuracy (around 80% in one recent study [160]). Mouse cursor movements on SERPs and landing pages can also be used to estimate satisfaction [106, 121]. For example, good abandonment (the positive absence of clicks [176, 294]) can be tracked when users are shown the types of instant answers (stocks, weather, etc.) that we mentioned earlier. Cursor movements on landing pages provide additional information about user engagement [106], extending beyond clicks and dwells, but require client-side logging to collect the data.

6.3   COMBINING METRICS

Metrics tend to be measured separately even though systems have multiple interrelated components that interact and affect the user experience [306]. The metrics may not even be correlated, e.g., [100] found only a weak correlation between measures of the three usability aspects: efficiency, effectiveness, and satisfaction. Given this low correlation, usability testing of computer systems for complex tasks should include measures of all three. This creates significant challenges in how to integrate and interpret these metrics.

Complex or integrated metrics combine multiple variables/different aspects of a complex system. The first attempt at combined metrics was "informativeness" [299], combining a subjective response about usefulness with the system's ability to present a ranked list of useful items to the user. Other attempts to create these metrics include factor analysis and structural equation modeling [306]. Toms [308] showed that factor analysis could find patterns in variables and extract a parsimonious set, e.g., map relevance to dimensions of system, user, and task. Structural equation modeling is more powerful, testing the fit between hypothesized and actual relationships, e.g., in the case of user engagement, [237] identified several actors (aesthetics, novelty, etc.) and their inter-relationships. Such complex metrics allow for more holistic evaluation of systems. However, the intuition behind them is unclear, as is the interpretation of the models that result. Consumer-oriented metrics such as the "net promoter score" (NPS) [249] attempt to encapsulate everything in a single metric reflecting whether a user would recommend a product to friends. The intuition behind the NPS metric is clear, but explaining the findings requires follow-up with customers (e.g., via surveys and focus groups).

We can also analyze the metrics to understand how well they match user behavior, relevance, and preferences [6, 309] and better understand their properties [50, 230]. Meta-analysis frameworks such as the intuitiveness test [261] analyze the extent to which metrics capture key properties to measure and align with user preferences in search task evaluation. Metric unanimity [10] suggests that if a system is superior along key dimensions, then this should be unanimously reflected in the metrics assessing those dimensions.

Combinations of metrics are commonly employed in the evaluation of task-oriented dialog systems, e.g., the PARADISE framework [321], which uses both dialog cost (e.g., the number of turns) and task success (i.e., whether the user problem is addressed). Task-oriented dialog systems can be assessed in several ways: (a) automatically (per component analysis of language understanding, dialog state tracking, policy optimization, language generation, etc.—see [301]); (b) simulations mimicking user behavior and enabling end-to-end evaluation (of task success rate, dialog length, average rewards, etc.), albeit with challenges in validation [243]; and (c) human evaluation, enabling metrics such as task success rate, irrelevant/redundant turn rate, satisfaction score, etc. Indirect evaluation involves using the simulator to engage in a conversation with the system and comparing different systems [300]. Direct evaluation involves people interacting with the system to complete a task and rate the experience, e.g., language understanding and response appropriateness are assessed in competitions such as the Multi-Domain Task-Completion Dialog Challenge [177].

6.4   FACTORS AFFECTING TASK PERFORMANCE

There are many factors task that affect performance, including intrinsic properties of the task itself (e.g., nature of the task [225], the topic [212], task difficulty [351], task complexity [54], and even task urgency [221]) as well as extrinsic properties such as user attributes (e.g., subject matter expertise [339], familiarity with task/topic [151]) and other external factors such as dependencies on others and organizational constraints. The nature of the task can have a considerable impact on user actions and task success. Two examples of non-traditional search tasks are slow search (searching without time constraints) and high-recall search (searching to find all relevant material). Vakkari [310] has developed a model integrating task complexity and user actions. Improving one's meta-cognitive skills in task planning and reflective assessment have been shown to improve task performance [40].

A key determinant of task performance, which we have not mentioned thus far in this subsection, is the support offered by the system for the task. In the next section, we will dive into some examples of system support and the metrics used to evaluate task performance. To evaluate these systems properly, it is insufficient to only perform component-level analysis with isolation and control variables at a specific point in time. We also need holistic task-based evaluation metrics [18]. We will discuss both component and holistic metrics briefly for each of the four case studies. In some cases, the component metrics serve as full or partial proxies for the holistic metrics.

6.5   CASE STUDIES

We now present four case studies drawn from our own evaluations of systems that offer different types of task support for various search and recommendation scenarios. The differences in functionality and desired outcome mean that different metrics are required to understand the effectiveness of the task support that each of these systems provide. The case studies are in the following.

- **Intelligent notifications:** A mechanism in a popular operating system presenting interruptive task reminders to users, with the aim that those reminders be non-redundant (i.e., not for tasks that are already completed).

- **Skill discovery:** An intelligent assistant capability that promotes skill discovery, suggesting relevant skills to users based on their current or future context. This is especially useful on headless devices (without displays) such as smart speakers, which cannot easily convey their functionality to users.

- **Contextual search:** A search engine functionality for improving the relevance of search results based on the task context, including previous searches, both recent (within-session) and historic (long-term), and other signals, e.g., location and reading level.

- **Conversational systems:** A novel type of multi-modal support for helping users complete complex tasks (e.g., with recipe preparation), spanning multiple devices simultaneously and capitalizing on their complementary strengths.

For each case study, we briefly describe the scenario and present the holistic and component metrics that were used to evaluate task performance. The case studies illustrate the compromises that are often necessary when performing task-based evaluation in operational systems,

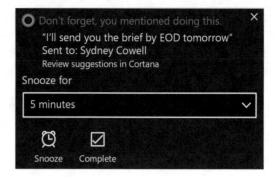

Figure 6.6: Screenshot of Microsoft Windows notification pop-up showing the task (commitment) extracted email and the options available to the user, including marking the task as complete. The presence and timing of these "mark complete" actions in retrospective log data has been used as weak labels to train machine-learned models for auto-detection of task completion [342].

where telemetry data may be voluminous but narrowly scoped to specific applications and scenarios.

6.5.1   INTELLIGENT NOTIFICATIONS

This first case study is focused on intelligent notifications in Microsoft Windows, where the operating system provides interruptive notifications (shown in Figure 6.6) for pending tasks. Tasks in this case are commitments that the user has made in email (e.g., "I will send the report by end of the day"). Supporting task retention addresses well-known limitations in human memory [171] and can be combined with context-sensitive reminders [141] and attention-sensitive alerts [17] to support prospective remembering. The primary aim is to inform the user of these tasks while not suggesting tasks that they have already completed—that would be redundant and could cause frustration.

As shown in Figure 6.6, the notification experience lets users mark tasks as complete with the "mark complete" affordance. However, if the user has already completed the task by the time the notification appears, by then it is too late, the user has already been interrupted. We take can these "mark complete" (weak supervision) signals when they do happen as a source of training data for machine-learned models to recognize completion events (even just based on elapsed time from creation to completion) and suppress notifications, auto-deprecate tasks, and so on. In some earlier work, we used anonymized Cortana logs to build accurate machine learned models to auto-detect task completion [342]. Given the availability of such functionality, the question is what are the best metrics to use to evaluate its effectiveness.

When deploying this in practice, the best (but unobservable) holistic measure would be user satisfaction related to the fewer redundant interrupts. While we could ask users about this directly, that is cumbersome and faces challenges in uptake. Satisfaction is a holistic measure that captures overall perceptions of the interruption experience with the intelligent system. It is difficult to measure directly, especially without the ability to ask users, and because we are focused on the *absence* of notifications, making it more difficult to solicit user feedback. To approximate this, we can use an offline proxy for user satisfaction, namely the accuracy of the pending task detection, defined as the fraction of notifications for truly pending tasks. Online measures of the fraction of tasks marked immediately as complete (implying redundancy) may also be appropriate. The underlying assumption is that users will be more satisfied if they are interrupted less often for already-completed tasks.

6.5.2   SKILL DISCOVERY

The next case study focuses on skill discovery in digital assistants (in this case, Microsoft Cortana), ensuring that users are aware of assistant capabilities. Skills are applications accessible by digital assistants to help complete specific tasks. This is an acute issue in headless devices, such as smart speakers, which can lack displays. Examples of these systems including the Amazon Echo[2] and the Google Home[3] devices. When interacting with such systems, users can be unaware of what intelligent assistants can do, lessening their effectiveness and hindering task completion.

We developed contextual skill recommendation models to suggest the right skill(s) to users at the right time, based on user context. This can be done proactively, if a reasonable (unobtrusive) user experience could be defined for that, or reactively, e.g., on demand in response to user requests such as "help me now!" We framed this as a ranking problem and learned to rank skills based on skill usage (in this case, previous skill invocations) [334]. We found that adding different features had different effects: adding context (time and place) boosted precision, while adding personal features boosted recall (see Figure 6.7).

The ideal holistic metrics would be engagement and task success, and aspects of those could be tracked in a deployed system over time (i.e., were the suggested skills actually used in practice and did users complete more tasks as a result?). Depending on the instrumentation available, this may be feasible. In our offline experiments to evaluate the models, we needed a proxy for task success. Since the skill ranking is so pivotal in determining whether users found the right skill and were ultimately successful, we focused on the component-level precision-recall of the recommendation model to generate the suggested skills, using previously logged skill invocations as (a weak) ground truth.

6.5.3   CONTEXTUAL SEARCH

The third case study we will consider is contextual search in the Microsoft Bing search engine [336]. Over several years, we developed many contextual search capabilities, including those

---

[2]https://www.amazon.com/echo
[3]https://store.google.com/us/category/connected_home

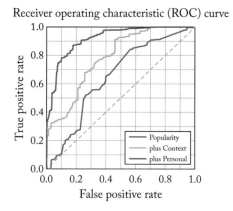
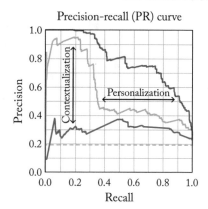

Figure 6.7: Receiver operating characteristic and precision-recall curves showing effect of contextualization and personalization for contextual skill recommendation. Results show that combining signal sources improves performance and that context boosts precision (light blue line) and personalization boosts recall (red line). Figure adapted from [334].

based on user location [38], reading level [75], previous queries from the same user (both short- and long-term) [39], from other users in the same cohort [358], and from other users attempting similar tasks [338]. These contextual features enable the search system to understand more aspects of the active search task and better rank the search results for that task.

Given the user and task effects discussed earlier, the ideal ground truth labels in this context are personalized, i.e., what content does the user in this context need to complete their task? We trained and evaluated models that used personalized judgments, mined from search logs and spanning multiple queries, to better capture task success per user. To do this, we used context-sensitive labels and metrics derived from clicks and context, including using characteristics of the clicks (e.g., satisfied click, last click, only click) as a way to define graded relevance judgments and capture some of the essence of task completion [39].

The ideal holistic metric would be fraction of users' tasks that actually got completed by using the search engine. In reality, since we can only observe queries and clicks in a search engine, we focused on a component-level analysis of the ranking model, using standard relevance metrics (e.g., MAP) as an offline proxy for task success and tracked other similar metrics (session success, utility, etc. [207]) in online scorecards. The results from offline tests (summarized in Figure 6.8) showed that taking features from the union of short- and long-term search histories led to the best contextual ranking performance in our offline experiments.

6.5.4   CONVERSATIONAL SYSTEMS

The final case study focuses on conversational systems, specifically multi-device experiences (MDX) [340]. The use of multiple digital devices to support people's daily activities has long been

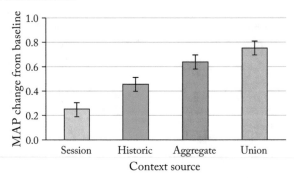

Figure 6.8: Changes in MAP from using different personal data sources for contextual search. Leveraging both short-term (session-level) and long-term histories yields the best result ranking performance. Figure adapted from [39].

Figure 6.9: Example multi-device setup, with an Apple iPad and an Amazon Echo being used simultaneously to complete a complex task (recipe preparation) powered by the multi-device experiences (MDX) service from Microsoft Research [340].

discussed [331]. Cross-device experiences (CDXs) and MDXs have been discussed in the literature on interaction design, human factors, and pervasive and ubiquitous computing [86, 272]. We created a cloud-based service that enables multiple devices with complementary capabilities to be brought together simultaneously (e.g., smart speaker plus smartphone) to support users in completing a task. Figures 6.9 and 6.10 show an example multi-device setup and a high-level schematic of MDX.

The focus was on helping users with complex tasks, targeting recipe preparation initially. The system had many components, with models for speech recognition, intent understanding,

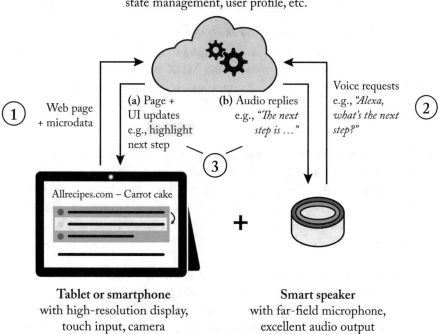

Cloud AI Service
Azure web service with AI for intent
understanding and question-answering plus
state management, user profile, etc.

① Web page + microdata

(a) Page + UI updates e.g., highlight next step

(b) Audio replies e.g., *"The next step is …"*

Voice requests e.g., *"Alexa, what's the next step?"* ②

③

Allrecipes.com – Carrot cake

+

Tablet or smartphone
with high-resolution display,
touch input, camera

Smart speaker
with far-field microphone,
excellent audio output

Figure 6.10: High-level low schematic for the MDX service, illustrating the primary components (including the cloud-based artificial intelligence (AI) backend that powers the multi-device experience), the interaction flow, and multi-modal interactions (in this case speech and touch). The MDX service can scale to any number of devices spanning modalities. Figure adapted from [340].

question answering, and stepwise recommendations (e.g., offering resource suggestions for the current step [236]), all of which interact to create the user experience. Metrics includes holistic and component level metrics—in this case, both of which are observable, meaning that proxies are not as necessary as in the other case studies. The holistic metrics included time on task and the number of dialog turns (effort). Component metrics included the correctness of the question answering, the word error rate of the speech recognition, and the accuracy of the intent understanding. The true challenge lies in bringing these metrics together to tell a consistent story about system performance and in setting thresholds for these metrics to help decide whether they meet a sufficient quality standards for the full system to be deployable in production.

6.6   CHALLENGES IN EVALUATION

It is apparent from the topics we have covered in this chapter thus far that evaluation of task-based systems is challenging. There are several reasons for this, including the following.

- **Task-based systems can be highly complex.** It can be difficult to attribute a task outcome to one component and it is challenging to model component-to-component interactions. For example, returning to the MDX system in the previous section, there may be components for speech recognition, intent understanding, question answering, and stepwise recommendation, all of which interact and can cause compounding errors.

- **Task activity is often unobservable**, both in terms of the process in completing the task and completion event itself. Many task-related activities are invisible to systems and are not archived for later analysis or modeling. Users can be reluctant to explicitly indicate progress or task completion, making it difficult to collect labeled data. Recent progress in weak supervision (learning based on proxy signals) can help address this shortcoming [285].

- **Task completion spans applications and devices.** Focusing on a single application (search engine, recommender system) or device (personal computer, smartphone) is too limited—we need more visibility across applications and devices. We need to evaluate task performance across applications and devices, weaving together activity from these different sources with consent to build holistic models of task activity.

- **Metric overload**, especially for complex systems/task scenarios. Using different metrics may lead to different system orderings. It is important to prioritize the metrics and be clear on the story they tell collectively (either a set of metrics or a single integrated metric). Relying on any one metric can lead to a biased perspective and result in poor downstream decisions.

- **Reliance on third-party labels for machine learning and data analytics.** Any classification of tasks or activities with a taxonomy by third parties is difficult [258]. First-party labeling is more reliable, albeit cumbersome for users to provide. This data can be collected through periodic recollections [139, 153] or in situ during task completion (e.g., using ESM [187]).

- **Task data stored but unavailable.** Task data may be recorded but, given privacy considerations, customer data may not be visible to researchers and system designers (so-called "eyes off" access). While machine-learned models can still be developed on these data (e.g., using methods such as differential privacy [1]), it is challenging to debug these algorithms or task-based systems more broadly, given limited insight into the

Capture-Organize ←——————————————————→ Achieve ——————→ Analyze

Figure 6.11: Task management personas derived from interviews and surveys with users of the Wunderlist to-do application. There are five such personas: collector, event planner, tomorrow planner, daily doer, and analyzer—focused to different degrees on capturing-organizing their task management activities, achieving their goals, and analyzing their task progress. It is important for system developers to understand task management personas such as these (including what fraction of users are in each and what fraction of the time users spend in each persona). Also, users can assume multiple personas over time. Credit: Carina Stefes.

tasks encountered. Small-scale studies with consenting users may be the only way to obtain "eyes on" data for development and evaluation purposes.

- **Task factors are not codified**. There are many factors that affect task performance but are not readily available to experimenters and system designers. We need to find ways to consider task difficulty, etc. in system evaluations. We also need to report task performance for different task management personas. Figure 6.11 has an example of a set of task management personas developed at Microsoft, based on an analysis of the Wunderlist task management application customer feedback and interviews. For evaluation purposes, personas such as these can help better understand the context around when task-based search and assistance is performing well and when it is underperforming.

These are just some examples of the types of challenges that we face when evaluating task-based search and recommendation systems. Of course, many of these challenges are also research opportunities and need to be explored in future work.

6.7   SUMMARY

There are a few key points to note before we conclude. The evaluation of task-based systems is important but is also challenging, for many reasons. There are many missing signals about the task itself (including complexity, urgency, and status) and about the user (including their expertise and task/topic familiarity). Focusing on activity within a single application, such as search, offers a myopic view. One way to better understand the task is to triangulate signals from multiple applications, with clear consent from users. As we showed in the case studies, each scenario has its own task setup, each with their own metrics and desired metric values. Careful thought is required in identifying complementary metrics and setting targets per application. Focusing on a single metric is often insufficient. We need to examine metrics together on scorecards and develop *intepretable* combined/integrated metrics. Collectively, metrics tell a story, but how easy that is to discern depends on reliable interpretation by skilled and experienced experimenters.

We have intentionally focused on holistic metrics in this chapter (given their broad applicability) and much less on evaluation methodologies, even though the two are inextricably linked. This includes the realism of any prescribed tasks (e.g., simulated work tasks [44]), the experimental setting, participants, baselines, and so on. Also, much of the discussion in this chapter has been focused on task execution, but task planning and reflective assessment (both meta-activities) are auxiliary processes related to task performance [291], as is the downstream utility of any information obtained during task completion.

It is clear that we need more research on complex/integrated metrics to handle the complex systems that support task completion. Beyond creating these metrics, we also need clear intuition and clear guidelines for how these metrics should be interpreted and used (and they will likely be highly application specific anyway). This is already an active area of study in online experimentation [162]. Continued research on using established models of information seeking behavior to inspect and evaluate the complex search systems is also an important direction [352]. We also need more investment in shared resources/datasets for task-based evaluation. The repository of tasks created by Wildemuth et al. [349][4] is one example of potentially useful task resources that can drive research in this area and help enable cross-experiment comparability, as has been advocated for from the early days of TREC [169].

---

[4]https://ils.unc.edu/searchtasks/search.php

CHAPTER 7

Conclusions and Future Directions

In the last chapter of this book, we will take an opportunity to not only summarize what we covered, but also reflect on previous chapters and consider where we go from here. It is that latter part that excites us most because the primary purpose of this book is not to simply synthesize existing research, but use that prior research to form a foundation for future research and development.

7.1 CONCLUSIONS

We have covered a lot of ground in the emerging area of task-based search and recommendation. It is clear that task assistance in the context of search and recommendation is a important domain that needs more study. There are a few key conclusions from this book.

First and foremost, we have learned that search and recommendation systems (also referred to as IR systems) should help their users accomplish tasks. This lesson is neither new nor unsupported. Scholars have argued for this for decades. What we continue to see is the evidence and argument for why this is a very important problem to address despite the phenomenal successes with our current IR systems. More importantly, the notion of such systems here goes beyond keyword-based retrieval and collaborative filtering, to include many recent and emerging approaches and applications. These include question-answering, conversational assistants, and contextual recommendation systems. We explored this notion in Chapter 1 as we considered a couple of scenarios that illustrate how task information can be useful in better fulfilling what a user wants to accomplish through an information interaction session, even when they are not very clear or articulate.

Given that there has been a tremendous amount of emphasis on understanding and addressing an information seeker's tasks, the literature is filled with frameworks and models for extracting task information and representing tasks in various situations. Chapter 2 highlighted some of these works. One important case we saw was with regards to explicit expression of tasks. This is quite frequent as many people use to-do applications, but not as well addressed because we often do not consider a to-do item as a task that can be accomplished through an IR system. However, as we saw in that chapter, we have an opportunity to do just that—taking someone's explicitly addressed task and help them accomplish it, whether it is through a search system, some other systems, or a combination of them. As more applications become integrated and our workflows get more complex, streamlining our tasks, the applications where we can take actions, and how we can get things done becomes a very important opportunity.

Beyond that special case of considering a task, we moved our attention to what is more widely studied in the literature—extracting and using task information from behavioral and other signals. As reported in Chapter 3, scholars have studied task in the context of task topic ("what" aspect) and intention ("why" aspect) to develop a comprehensive understanding of a user's task. These basic constructs of an information interaction—task topic, task type, user intent, and user behaviors—are often studied separately from one another, but we also saw how they are connected, and more importantly, how they could help us develop a more comprehensive understanding of that episode of information interaction. It is important to note that often theoretically appealing ideas are harder to operationalize in practice. It is not always easy or even possible to obtain a user's intent or ask them about their perceptions regarding their interactions with an IR system. Therefore, one has to be careful about assuming these signals being given, especially if they are interested in scaling and generalizing their solutions.

In Chapter 4, we saw that task and user characteristics contribute significantly to task behavior and task performance. We need more research on integrating aspects of these characteristics into task modeling and evaluation. Task information can be inferred from user behaviors, content analysis, and contextual understanding, where context can be defined broadly, spanning both virtual and physical. There are clear privacy implications in making these inferences and before leveraging these signals for this purpose, user consent needs to be obtained.

Then, in Chapter 5, we looked at how we could apply task knowledge or how tasks can be supported in various IR situations. Systems can support tasks in many ways, e.g., recommendations for e-commerce is one such example, and we offered additional examples in the case studies we presented. As we dig deeper into the literature, we find that while there are lots of works explaining how task information is important (Chapter 2), how it is used in IR (Chapter 3), and how we could extract knowledge about tasks (Chapter 4), there is not nearly as much work related to using task knowledge in mainstream IR applications. In other words, there is a great potential here to use the foundational works done so far and apply them to improving exiting IR systems and envisioning new kinds of them.

Finally, in Chapter 6 we showed that the evaluation of task-based systems is challenging, especially given limited information about users and tasks. We really need to consider a range of metrics, per application, both holistic (tied to the overall user experience) and per component (tied to the performance of individual elements of the system)—as well as *interpretable*, integrated metrics. We only touched on some salient metrics in Chapter 6. Other metrics are also important: learning, creativity (short- and long-term), and many more.

7.2   FUTURE DIRECTIONS

An obvious question after all this is where are we going next? It is clear that the future is bright for task-based search and recommendation. There are many directions that research in this area can take, and many opportunities to leverage advances in areas such as AI and ML to better understand intent and anticipate future needs.

Going forward, there are several opportunities. We will highlight just a few here.

Systems need to better support end-to-end task completion. They need to do so through seamless integration with existing tools and cross-application support (no more task silos, where tasks are trapped within specific applications (e.g., in specialized to-do applications such as Todoist and Microsoft To Do) when in reality they span applications.[1]) Task fabrics spanning applications and operating systems are needed to ensure users have access to tasks from anywhere and signals from these sources are available for machine learning tasks such as contextual task prioritization. Beyond supporting task planning and organization (something that has already been studied extensively [35], AI can help in other well-known task phases, namely task capture and execution [9]. Short tasks such as action items have already been automatically extracted from email [37, 234].

We need to better understand the tasks being done, both for system design and for evaluation. We need to better model task intents. There has been research in this area in the context of email [327]. We could also create a semantic task representation such as "task2vec," a vector representation of task intent, trained, for example, based on task co-occurrence in usage data. We also need more signals on task progress and task completion (based on both activity, e.g., visiting physical locations where tasks get completed, and content, e.g., replying to emails with the text "Done" or "Please see attached"), and more triangulation of those signals with other contextual data (with user consent) to improve confidence in any inferences or forecasts we make.

Focusing on task completion is vital. Support for tasks is currently fragmented. For example, search engines support finding information, but not full tasks. Task management applications capture tasks and serve reminders but do not facilitate completion. Task completion is really the last mile in search interaction [333]. We can turn search engines into task completion engines [18]. We can start by supporting completion when we already know the task (e.g., to-do tasks). An example of this might be so-called "task2search" [280], i.e., finding the tasks that search engines can directly help with and providing an affordance within to-do applications to engage with the search engine to complete the task. Myers et al. [235] designed a system to aid in repetitive tasks. *TaskGenies* generated action plans decomposing tasks into small, actionable sub-tasks [163]. Meanwhile, Stumpf et al. [296] and Kiseleva at al. [158] focused on interpreting user goals and then providing the necessary resources. We also need to evaluate how well the systems support taskflows/end-to-end task completion and whether we can recommend taskflows/make task-based suggestions to users. One way is to learn these flows from logs combined with semantic labeling [286, 304].

Context is important. Context-aware recommendation systems [108, 283, 335] aim to leverage contextual information, such as location [360] and/or time [367], to improve the qual-

---

[1]There have already been some discussion of related ideas under the umbrella of activity-centric rather than application-centric computing [326].

ity of the suggestions they offer. This can be used for applications such as travel recommenda-tions [159] and context-sensitive reminding [141]. By combining location with time informa-tion, context-aware task management systems assist users by suggesting the right tasks at the right time [154, 251] and batching together tasks that can be done at the same times and/or places. Recent research has sought to understand the physical locations where people perform certain types of tasks and activities [36]. Contextual factors such as busyness have been shown to impact the effectiveness of the task assistance and the extent to which people depend on it [143, 175]. The role of context in task management needs to be better understood and context needs to be better utilized in task support.

Tasks are not first-class objects in many systems. Only aspects of them (e.g., retrieval, sug-gestion) are supported and users must stitch together the other aspects to complete the tasks, especially in general purpose systems such as search engines (in specialized systems, task work-flows are often well established). Tasks could be supported more directly in general purpose systems, e.g., via guided tours and trails mined from search logs [112, 286] or from subject matter experts [364]. Reusable components (e.g., guided tour generation and user experiences for trail blazing (authoring trails) and trail following) could also be developed and shared across general purpose applications and those meant to help users tackle specific tasks.

As noted several places in this book, task knowledge can also help us take conceptual and pragmatic leaps in emerging area of intelligent assistants. This is particularly true for conver-sational systems. Knowing the task behind a user's request can help with better fulfilment of that request, but could also allow an agent to have more productive multi-turn conversation. This is currently difficult for these agents as they are built to treat each interaction in isolation with only shallow-level connection between two subsequent requests. Having a context-aware, task-aware, and multi-turn meaningful conversation could fundamentally change the field of intelligent assistants. These assistants or agents can also use the same information to provide proactive recommendations and help address the "people don't know what they don't know" challenge.

These are just some examples of the types of areas that could be explored—the research opportunities in task-based search and assistance space are plentiful. As a community, we need to find ways to drive more research in this area, through shared datasets, living laboratories, data challenges, TREC tracks, or other mechanisms such as workshops. One thing is clear: without sufficient task assistance, people will continue to tackle complex tasks on their own, with associated inefficiencies and sub-optimal outcomes. Task-based search and recommendation systems will help them overcome these challenges.

Bibliography

[1] Abadi, M., Chu, A., Goodfellow, I., McMahan, H. B., Mironov, I., Talwar, K., and Zhang, L. Deep learning with differential privacy. In *Proc. of the ACM SIGSAC Conference on Computer and Communications Security*, pages 308–318, 2016. DOI: 10.1145/2976749.2978318 96

[2] Agichtein, E., White, R. W., Dumais, S. T., and Bennett, P. N. Search, interrupted: Understanding and predicting search task continuation. In *Proc. of the ACM SIGIR Conference on Research and Development in Information Retrieval*, pages 315–324, 2012. DOI: 10.1145/2348283.2348328 63

[3] Agosti, M., Fuhr, N., Toms, E., and Vakkari, P. Evaluation methodologies in information retrieval Dagstuhl seminar 13441. *ACM SIGIR Forum 48*, 1:36–41, 2014. DOI: 10.1145/2641383.2641390 78

[4] Agosto, D. E. and Hughes-Hassell, S. Toward a model of the everyday life information needs of urban teenagers, part 2: Empirical model. *Journal of the American Society for Information Science and Technology 57*, 11:1418–1426, 2006. DOI: 10.1002/asi.20452 14

[5] Ai, Q., Zhang, Y., Bi, K., Chen, X., and Croft, W. B. Learning a hierarchical embedding model for personalized product search. In *Proc. of the ACM SIGIR Conference on Research and Development in Information Retrieval*, pages 645–654, 2017. DOI: 10.1145/3077136.3080813 71

[6] Albahem, A., Spina, D., Scholer, F., and Cavedon, L. Meta-evaluation of dynamic search: How do metrics capture topical relevance, diversity and user effort? In *Proc. of the European Conference on Information Retrieval*, pages 607–620, 2019. DOI: 10.1007/978-3-030-15712-8_39 89

[7] Albert, W. and Tullis, T. *Measuring the User Experience: Collecting, Analyzing, and Presenting Usability Metrics*. Morgan Kaufmann, 2013. 78

[8] Allan, J., Croft, B., Moffat, A., and Sanderson, M. Frontiers, challenges, and opportunities for information retrieval: Report from swirl 2012 the second strategic workshop on information retrieval in lorne. *ACM SIGIR Forum 46*, 1:2–32, 2012. DOI: 10.1145/2215676.2215678 7

[9] Allen, D. *Getting Things Done: The Art of Stress-Free Productivity*. Penguin, 2015. 13, 101

[10] Amigó, E., Spina, D., and Carrillo-de Albornoz, J. An axiomatic analysis of diversity evaluation metrics: Introducing the rank-biased utility metric. In *Proc. of the ACM SIGIR Conference on Research and Development in Information Retrieval*, pages 625–634, 2018. DOI: 10.1145/3209978.3210024 89

[11] Arguello, J. Predicting search task difficulty. In *Proc. of the European Conference on Information Retrieval*, pages 88–99, 2014. DOI: 10.1007/978-3-319-06028-6_8 56

[12] Athukorala, K., Głowacka, D., Jacucci, G., Oulasvirta, A., and Vreeken, J. Is exploratory search different? A comparison of information search behavior for exploratory and lookup tasks. *Journal of the Association for Information Science and Technology 67*, 11:2635–2651, 2016. DOI: 10.1002/asi.23617 50, 56, 60

[13] Aula, A., Khan, R. M., and Guan, Z. How does search behavior change as search becomes more difficult? In *Proc. of the ACM SIGCHI Conference on Human Factors in Computing Systems*, pages 35–44, 2010. DOI: 10.1145/1753326.1753333 16, 56

[14] Awadallah, A. H., White, R. W., Pantel, P., Dumais, S. T., and Wang, Y.-M. Supporting complex search tasks. In *Proc. of the ACM CIKM Conference on Information and Knowledge Management*, pages 829–838, 2014. DOI: 10.1145/2661829.2661912 12, 22, 63

[15] Azzopardi, L., Kelly, D., and Brennan, K. How query cost affects search behavior. In *Proc. of the ACM SIGIR Conference on Research and Development in Information Retrieval*, pages 23–32, 2013. DOI: 10.1145/2484028.2484049 82

[16] Azzopardi, L., Thomas, P., and Craswell, N. Measuring the utility of search engine result pages: An information foraging based measure. In *Proc. of the ACM SIGIR Conference on Research and Development in Information Retrieval*, pages 605–614, 2018. DOI: 10.1145/3209978.3210027 83

[17] Bailey, B. P. and Konstan, J. A. On the need for attention-aware systems: Measuring effects of interruption on task performance, error rate, and affective state. *Computers in Human Behavior 22*, 4:685–708, 2006. DOI: 10.1016/j.chb.2005.12.009 91

[18] Balog, K. Task-completion engines: A vision with a plan. In *Proc. of the Supporting Complex Search Task Workshop*, 2015. 90, 101

[19] Balog, K., Kelly, L., and Schuth, A. Head first: Living labs for ad hoc search evaluation. In *Proc. of the ACM CIKM Conference on Information and Knowledge Management*, pages 1815–1818, 2014. DOI: 10.1145/2661829.2661962 77

[20] Banovic, N., Brant, C., Mankoff, J., and Dey, A. Proactivetasks: The short of mobile device use sessions. In *Proc. of the International Conference on Human-Computer Interaction with Mobile Devices and Services*, pages 243–252, 2014. DOI: 10.1145/2628363.2628380 14

[21] Baraglia, R., Cacheda, F., Carneiro, V., Formoso, V., Perego, R., and Silvestri, F. Search shortcuts: Driving users towards their goals. In *Proc. of the International Conference on the World Wide Web*, pages 1073–1074, 2009. DOI: 10.1145/1526709.1526862 63

[22] Basilico, J. and Hofmann, T. Unifying collaborative and content-based filtering. In *Proc. of the International Conference on Machine Learning*, p. 9, 2004. DOI: 10.1145/1015330.1015394 12

[23] Bates, M. J. The design of browsing and berrypicking techniques for the online search interface. *Online Review 13*, 5:407–424, 1989. DOI: 10.1108/eb024320 11, 18, 79

[24] Bates, M. J. Where should the person stop and the information search interface start? *Information Processing and Management 26*, 5:575–591, 1990. DOI: 10.1016/0306-4573(90)90103-9 75

[25] Beaulieu, M. Experiments on interfaces to support query expansion. *Journal of Documentation 53*, 1:8–15, 1997. DOI: 10.1108/eum0000000007187 78

[26] Beheshti, J., Cole, C., Abuhimed, D., and Lamoureux, I. Tracking middle school students' information behavior via Kuhlthau's ISP model: Temporality. *Journal of the Association for Information Science and Technology 66*, 5:943–960, 2015. DOI: 10.1002/asi.23230 17

[27] Belkin, N., Bogers, T., Kamps, J., Kelly, D., Koolen, M., and Yilmaz, E. Second workshop on supporting complex search tasks. In *Proc. of the ACM CHIIR Conference on Human Information Interaction and Retrieval*, pages 433–435, 2017. DOI: 10.1145/3020165.3022163 3, 8

[28] Belkin, N. J. Anomalous states of knowledge as a basis for information retrieval. *Canadian Journal of Information Science 5*, 1:133–143, 1980. 2, 17, 53

[29] Belkin, N. J. A methodology for taking account of user tasks, goals and behavior for design of computerized library catalogs. *ACM SIGCHI Bulletin 23*, 1:61–65, 1991. DOI: 10.1145/122672.122687 21

[30] Belkin, N. J. Intelligent information retrieval: Whose intelligence? *Herausforderungen an die Informationswirtschaft 96*, 25, 1996. 19

[31] Belkin, N. J. Some (what) grand challenges for information retrieval. *ACM SIGIR Forum 42*, 1:47–54, 2008. DOI: 10.1145/1394251.1394261 1, 3

[32] Belkin, N. J. People, interacting with information. *ACM SIGIR Forum 49*, 2:13–27, 2016. DOI: 10.1145/2888422.2888424 1, 3

[33] Belkin, N. J., Clarke, C. L., Gao, N., Kamps, J., and Karlgren, J. Report on the SIGIR workshop on "entertain me": Supporting complex search tasks. *ACM SIGIR Forum 45*, 2:51–59, 2012. DOI: 10.1145/2093346.2093354 8

[34] Belkin, N. J., Cole, M., and Liu, J. A model for evaluation of interactive information retrieval. In *Proc. of the SIGIR Workshop on the Future of IR Evaluation*, pages 7–8, 2009. 86

[35] Bellotti, V., Dalal, B., Good, N., Flynn, P., Bobrow, D. G., and Ducheneaut, N. What a to-do: Studies of task management towards the design of a personal task list manager. In *Proc. of the ACM SIGCHI Conference on Human Factors in Computing Systems*, pages 735–742, 2004. DOI: 10.1145/985692.985785 13, 85, 101

[36] Benetka, J. R., Krumm, J., and Bennett, P. N. Understanding context for tasks and activities. In *Proc. of the CHIIR Conference on Conference Human Information Interaction and Retrieval*, pages 133–142, 2019. DOI: 10.1145/3295750.3298929 102

[37] Bennett, P. N. and Carbonell, J. Detecting action-items in e-mail. In *Proc. of the ACM SIGIR Conference on Research and Development in Information Retrieval*, pages 585–586, 2005. DOI: 10.1145/1076034.1076140 101

[38] Bennett, P. N., Radlinski, F., White, R. W., and Yilmaz, E. Inferring and using location metadata to personalize web search. In *Proc. of the ACM SIGIR Conference on Research and Development in Information Retrieval*, pages 135–144, 2011. DOI: 10.1145/2009916.2009938 87, 93

[39] Bennett, P. N., White, R. W., Chu, W., Dumais, S. T., Bailey, P., Borisyuk, F., and Cui, X. Modeling the impact of short-and long-term behavior on search personalization. In *Proc. of the ACM SIGIR Conference on Research and Development in Information Retrieval*, pages 185–194, 2012. DOI: 10.1145/2348283.2348312 87, 93, 94

[40] Biggs, J. The role of metacognition in enhancing learning. *Australian Journal of Education 32*, 2:127–138, 1988. DOI: 10.1177/000494418803200201 90

[41] Blei, D. M., Ng, A. Y., and Jordan, M. I. Latent dirichlet allocation. *Journal of Machine Learning Research 3*, pages 993–1022, 2003. DOI: 10.1109/asru.2015.7404785 23

[42] Bloom, B. S. *Taxonomy of Educational Objectives. vol. 1: Cognitive Domain.* pages 20–24, New York, McKay, 1956. 20

[43] Boltz, M. G., Kupperman, C., and Dunne, J. The role of learning in remembered duration. *Memory and Cognition 26*, 5:903–921, 1998. DOI: 10.3758/bf03201172 82

[44] Borlund, P.   Experimental components for the evaluation of interactive information retrieval systems.   *Journal of Documentation 56*, 1:71–90, 2000. DOI: 10.1108/eum0000000007110 76, 98

[45] Borlund, P. The IIR evaluation model: A framework for evaluation of interactive information retrieval systems. *Information Research 8*, 3:8–3, 2003. 32

[46] Broder, A. A taxonomy of web search. *ACM SIGIR Forum 36*, 2:3–10, 2002. DOI: 10.1145/792550.792552 33

[47] Brovman, Y. M., Jacob, M., Srinivasan, N., Neola, S., Galron, D., Snyder, R., and Wang, P. Optimizing similar item recommendations in a semi-structured marketplace to maximize conversion. In *Proc. of the ACM RecSys Conference on Recommender Systems*, pages 199–202, 2016. DOI: 10.1145/2959100.2959166 87

[48] Bruza, P., McArthur, R., and Dennis, S. Interactive internet search: Keyword, directory and query reformulation mechanisms compared. In *Proc. of the ACM SIGIR Conference on Research and Development in Information Retrieval*, pages 280–287, 2000. DOI: 10.1145/345508.345598 78

[49] Budzianowski, P., Wen, T.-H., Tseng, B.-H., Casanueva, I., Ultes, S., Ramadan, O., and Gasic, M. Multiwoz-a large-scale multi-domain wizard-of-oz dataset for task-oriented dialogue modelling. In *Proc. of the Conference on Empirical Methods in Natural Language Processing*, pages 5016–5026, 2018. DOI: 10.18653/v1/d18-1547 86

[50] Busin, L. and Mizzaro, S. Axiometrics: An axiomatic approach to information retrieval effectiveness metrics. In *Proc. of the ACM ICTIR Conference on the Theory of Information Retrieval*, pages 22–29, 2013. DOI: 10.1145/2499178.2499182 89

[51] Byström, K. Approaches to task in contemporary information studies. In *Proc. of the International Conference on Conceptions of Library and Information Science*, 12:1–10, 2007. 2

[52] Byström, K. and Hansen, P. Work tasks as units for analysis in information seeking and retrieval studies. In *Proc. of the International Conference on Conceptions of Library and Information Science*, pages 239–251, 2002. 2, 14, 15, 51

[53] Byström, K. and Hansen, P. Conceptual framework for tasks in information studies. *Journal of the American Society for Information Science and Technology 56*, 10:1050–1061, 2005. DOI: 10.1002/asi.20197 2, 11, 14, 51

[54] Byström, K. and Järvelin, K. Task complexity affects information seeking and use. *Information Processing and Management 31*, 2:191–213, 1995. DOI: 10.1016/0306-4573(95)80035-r 11, 20, 89

[55] Cai, F., Liang, S., and De Rijke, M. Personalized document re-ranking based on Bayesian probabilistic matrix factorization. In *Proc. of the ACM SIGIR Conference on Research and Development in Information Retrieval*, pages 835–838, 2014. DOI: 10.1145/2600428.2609453 63

[56] Cao, H., Jiang, D., Pei, J., Chen, E., and Li, H. Towards context-aware search by learning a very large variable length hidden Markov model from search logs. In *Proc. of the International Conference on the World Wide Web*, pages 191–200, 2009. DOI: 10.1145/1526709.1526736 22, 64

[57] Cao, H., Jiang, D., Pei, J., He, Q., Liao, Z., Chen, E., and Li, H. Context-aware query suggestion by mining click-through and session data. In *Proc. of the ACM SIGKDD Conference on Knowledge Discovery and Data Mining*, pages 875–883, 2008. DOI: 10.1145/1401890.1401995 22

[58] Capra, R., Arguello, J., O'Brien, H., Li, Y., and Choi, B. The effects of manipulating task determinability on search behaviors and outcomes. In *Proc. of the ACM SIGIR Conference on Research and Development in Information Retrieval*, pages 445–454, 2018. DOI: 10.1145/3209978.3210047 11, 16, 21

[59] Capra, R., Arguello, J., and Zhang, Y. The effects of search task determinability on search behavior. In *Proc. of the European Conference on Information Retrieval*, pages 108–121, 2017. DOI: 10.1007/978-3-319-56608-5_9 21

[60] Card, S. K. *The Psychology of Human-Computer Interaction*. CRC Press, 2018. DOI: 10.1201/9780203736166' 78, 81

[61] Carterette, B., Clough, P., Hall, M., Kanoulas, E., and Sanderson, M. Evaluating retrieval over sessions: The TREC session track 2011–2014. In *Proc. of the ACM SIGIR Conference on Research and Development in Information Retrieval*, pages 685–688, 2016. DOI: 10.1145/2911451.2914675 72, 87

[62] Carterette, B., Kanoulas, E., Hall, M., and Clough, P. Overview of the TREC 2014 session track. *Technical Report*, Delaware University, Newark, 2014. 50

[63] Chapelle, O., Joachims, T., Radlinski, F., and Yue, Y. Large-scale validation and analysis of interleaved search evaluation. *ACM Transactions on Information Systems 30*, 1:1–41, 2012. DOI: 10.1145/2094072.2094078 76

[64] Chapelle, O., Metlzer, D., Zhang, Y., and Grinspan, P. Expected reciprocal rank for graded relevance. In *Proc. of the ACM CIKM Conference on Information and Knowledge Management*, pages 621–630, 2009. DOI: 10.1145/1645953.1646033 82

[65] Charnov, E. L. Optimal foraging, the marginal value theorem. *Theoretical Population Biology 9*, 2:129–136, 1976. DOI: 10.1016/0040-5809(76)90040-x 82

[66] Chaturvedi, A., Green, P. E., and Caroll, J. D. K-modes clustering. *Journal of Classification 18*, 1:35–55, 2001. DOI: 10.1007/s00357-001-0004-3 52

[67] Chen, H., Liu, X., Yin, D., and Tang, J. A survey on dialogue systems: Recent advances and new frontiers. *ACM SIGKDD Explorations Newsletter 19*, 2:25–35, 2017. DOI: 10.1145/3166054.3166058 84

[68] Chen, J., Liu, Y., Luo, C., Mao, J., Zhang, M., and Ma, S. Improving session search performance with a multi-MDP model. In *Proc. of the Asia Information Retrieval Symposium*, pages 45–59, 2018. DOI: 10.1007/978-3-030-03520-4_5 72

[69] Cheng, H.-T., Koc, L., Harmsen, J., Shaked, T., Chandra, T., Aradhye, H., Anderson, G., Corrado, G., Chai, W., Ispir, M., et al. Wide and deep learning for recommender systems. In *Proc. of the Workshop on Deep Learning for Recommender Systems*, pages 7–10, 2016. DOI: 10.1145/2988450.2988454 12

[70] Clarke, C. L., Freund, L., Smucker, M. D., and Yilmaz, E. Report on the SIGIR 2013 workshop on modeling user behavior for information retrieval evaluation. *ACM SIGIR Forum 47*, 2:84–95, 2013. DOI: 10.1145/2568388.2568403 8

[71] Clarke, C. L., Kolla, M., Cormack, G. V., Vechtomova, O., Ashkan, A., Büttcher, S., and MacKinnon, I. Novelty and diversity in information retrieval evaluation. In *Proc. of the ACM SIGIR Conference on Research and Development in Information Retrieval*, pages 659–666, 2008. DOI: 10.1145/1390334.1390446 79

[72] Clarke, C. L. and Smucker, M. D. Time well spent. In *Proc. of the Information Interaction in Context Symposium*, pages 205–214, 2014. DOI: 10.1145/2637002.2637026 81

[73] Cleverdon, C. The Cranfield tests on index language devices. *Aslib Proceedings 19*, 6:173–194, 1967. DOI: 10.1108/eb050097 76

[74] Cole, M. J., Hendahewa, C., Belkin, N. J., and Shah, C. User activity patterns during information search. *ACM Transactions on Information Systems 33*, 1:1–39, 2015. DOI: 10.1145/2699656 20, 29

[75] Collins-Thompson, K., Bennett, P. N., White, R. W., De La Chica, S., and Sontag, D. Personalizing web search results by reading level. In *Proc. of the ACM CIKM Conference on Information and Knowledge Management*, pages 403–412, 2011. DOI: 10.1145/2063576.2063639 93

[76] Collins-Thompson, K., Macdonald, C., Bennett, P., Diaz, F., and Voorhees, E. M. TREC 2014 web track overview. *Technical Report*, University of Michigan, Ann Arbor, 2015. 29

[77] Cooley, R., Mobasher, B., and Srivastava, J. Data preparation for mining world wide web browsing patterns. *Knowledge and Information Systems 1*, 1:5–32, 1999. DOI: 10.1007/bf03325089 22

[78] Cooper, W. S. Expected search length: A single measure of retrieval effectiveness based on the weak ordering action of retrieval systems. *American Documentation 19*, 1:30–41, 1968. DOI: 10.1002/asi.5090190108 84

[79] Cormack, G. V. and Lynam, T. R. Statistical precision of information retrieval evaluation. In *Proc. of the ACM SIGIR Conference on Research and Development in Information Retrieval*, pages 533–540, 2006. DOI: 10.1145/1148170.1148262 68

[80] Craswell, N. and Szummer, M. Random walks on the click graph. In *Proc. of the ACM SIGIR Conference on Research and Development in Information Retrieval*, pages 239–246, 2007. DOI: 10.1145/1277741.1277784 23

[81] Crescenzi, A., Kelly, D., and Azzopardi, L. Impacts of time constraints and system delays on user experience. In *Proc. of the ACM CHIIR Conference on Human Information Interaction and Retrieval*, pages 141–150, 2016. DOI: 10.1145/2854946.2854976 56

[82] Csikszentmihalyi, M. *Flow: The Psychology of Optimal Experience*. Harper and Row, 1990. 77, 82, 85

[83] Culpepper, J. S., Diaz, F., and Smucker, M. D. Research frontiers in information retrieval: Report from the third strategic workshop on information retrieval in lorne (SWIRL 2018). *ACM SIGIR Forum 52*, 1:34–90, 2018. DOI: 10.1145/3274784.3274788 21

[84] Czerwinski, M., Horvitz, E., and Wilhite, S. A diary study of task switching and interruptions. In *Proc. of the ACM SIGCHI Conference on Human Factors in Computing Systems*, pages 175–182, 2004. DOI: 10.1145/985692.985715 80

[85] Dervin, B. Sense-making theory and practice: An overview of user interests in knowledge seeking and use. *Journal of Knowledge Management 2*, 2:36–46, 1998. DOI: 10.1108/13673279810249369 2, 3, 17, 32, 33

[86] Dong, T., Churchill, E. F., and Nichols, J. Understanding the challenges of designing and developing multi-device experiences. In *Proc. of the ACM DIS Conference on Designing Interactive Systems*, pages 62–72, 2016. DOI: 10.1145/2901790.2901851 94

[87] Downey, D., Dumais, S., Liebling, D., and Horvitz, E. Understanding the relationship between searchers' queries and information goals. In *Proc. of the ACM CIKM Conference on Information and Knowledge Management*, pages 449–458, 2008. DOI: 10.1145/1458082.1458143 87

[88] Dumais, S. Evaluating IR in situ. In *Proc. of the SIGIR Workshop on the Future of IR Evaluation*, p. 2, 2009. 76

[89] Dumais, S. Task-based search: A search engine perspective. In *Proc. of the NSF Workshop on Task-Based Search*, 2013. 76, 79

[90] Dungs, S. and Fuhr, N. Advanced hidden Markov models for recognizing search phases. In *Proc. of the ACM ICTIR International Conference on the Theory of Information Retrieval*, pages 257–260, 2017. DOI: 10.1145/3121050.3121090 20

[91] Dunlop, M. D. Time, relevance and interaction modelling for information retrieval. *ACM SIGIR Forum 31*, pages 206–213, 1997. DOI: 10.1145/258525.258569 84

[92] Dupret, G. E. and Piwowarski, B. A user browsing model to predict search engine click data from past observations. In *Proc. of the ACM SIGIR Conference on Research and Development in Information Retrieval*, pages 331–338, 2008. DOI: 10.1145/1390334.1390392 77, 82

[93] Eickhoff, C., Teevan, J., White, R., and Dumais, S. Lessons from the journey: A query log analysis of within-session learning. In *Proc. of the ACM WSDM International Conference on Web Search and Data Mining*, pages 223–232, 2014. DOI: 10.1145/2556195.2556217 78

[94] Ellis, D. A behavioural approach to information retrieval system design. *Journal of Documentation 45*, 3:171–212, 1989. DOI: 10.1108/eb026843 17, 18

[95] Ellis, D. Modeling the information-seeking patterns of academic researchers: A grounded theory approach. *The Library Quarterly 63*, 4:469–486, 1993. DOI: 10.1086/602622 17

[96] Ellis, D., Cox, D., and Hall, K. A comparison of the information seeking patterns of researchers in the physical and social sciences. *Journal of Documentation 49*, 4:356–369, 1993. DOI: 10.1108/eb026919 17

[97] Feild, H. A., Allan, J., and Jones, R. Predicting searcher frustration. In *Proc. of the ACM SIGIR Conference on Research and Development in Information Retrieval*, pages 34–41, 2010. DOI: 10.1145/1835449.1835458 78

[98] Fox, S., Karnawat, K., Mydland, M., Dumais, S., and White, T. Evaluating implicit measures to improve web search. *ACM Transactions on Information Systems 23*, 2:147–168, 2005. DOI: 10.1145/1059981.1059982 79, 80, 88

[99] Freund, L. Exploiting task-document relations in support of information retrieval in the workplace. Ph.D. thesis, University of Toronto, 2008. DOI: 10.1145/1480506.1480529 21

[100] Frøkjær, E., Hertzum, M., and Hornbæk, K. Measuring usability: Are effectiveness, efficiency, and satisfaction really correlated? In *Proc. of the ACM SIGCHI Conference on Human Factors in Computing Systems*, pages 345–352, 2000. DOI: 10.1145/332040.332455 78, 88

[101] Fuhr, N. A probability ranking principle for interactive information retrieval. *Information Retrieval 11*, 3:251–265, 2008. DOI: 10.1007/s10791-008-9045-0 20

[102] Gäde, M., Hall, M. M., Huurdeman, H., Kamps, J., Koolen, M., Skove, M., Toms, E., and Walsh, D. Report on the first workshop on supporting complex search tasks. *ACM SIGIR Forum 49*, 1:50–56, 2015. DOI: 10.1145/2795403.2795415 8

[103] Ghosh, S., Rath, M., and Shah, C. Searching as learning: Exploring search behavior and learning outcomes in learning-related tasks. In *Proc. of the ACM CHIIR Conference on Human Information Interaction and Retrieval*, pages 22–31, 2018. DOI: 10.1145/3176349.3176386 20

[104] Graus, D., Bennett, P. N., White, R. W., and Horvitz, E. Analyzing and predicting task reminders. In *Proc. of the ACM UMAP Conference on User Modeling Adaptation and Personalization*, pages 7–15, 2016. DOI: 10.1145/2930238.2930239 13

[105] Grimes, C., Tang, D., and Russell, D. Query logs alone are not enough. In *WWW Workshop on Query Log Analysis: Social and Technological Changes*, 2007. 77

[106] Guo, Q. and Agichtein, E. Beyond dwell time: Estimating document relevance from cursor movements and other post-click searcher behavior. In *Proc. of the International Conference on the World Wide Web*, pages 569–578, 2012. DOI: 10.1145/2187836.2187914 88

[107] Hansen, P., Shah, C., and Klas, C.-P., Eds. *Collaborative Information Seeking—Best Practices, New Domains, New Thoughts*. Springer, 2015. 139

[108] Hariri, N., Mobasher, B., and Burke, R. Query-driven context aware recommendation. In *Proc. of the ACM RecSys Conference on Recommender Systems*, pages 9–16, 2013. DOI: 10.1145/2507157.2507187 101

[109] Hassan, A., Jones, R., and Klinkner, K. L. Beyond DCG: User behavior as a predictor of a successful search. In *Proc. of the ACM WSDM International Conference on Web Search and Data Mining*, pages 221–230, 2010. DOI: 10.1145/1718487.1718515 87

[110] Hassan, A., Shi, X., Craswell, N., and Ramsey, B. Beyond clicks: Query reformulation as a predictor of search satisfaction. In *Proc. of the ACM CIKM Conference on Information and Knowledge Management*, pages 2019–2028, 2013. DOI: 10.1145/2505515.2505682 63, 64

[111] Hassan, A., Song, Y., and He, L.-W. A task level metric for measuring web search satisfaction and its application on improving relevance estimation. In *Proc. of the ACM CIKM Conference on Information and Knowledge Management*, pages 125–134, 2011. DOI: 10.1145/2063576.2063599 88

[112] Hassan, A. and White, R. W. Task tours: Helping users tackle complex search tasks. In *Proc. of the ACM CIKM Conference on Information and Knowledge Management*, pages 1885–1889, 2012. DOI: 10.1145/2396761.2398537 12, 64, 102

[113] Hassan, A. and White, R. W. Personalized models of search satisfaction. In *Proc. of the ACM CIKM Conference on Information and Knowledge Management*, pages 2009–2018, 2013. DOI: 10.1145/2505515.2505681 88

[114] Hassan, A., White, R. W., Dumais, S. T., and Wang, Y.-M. Struggling or exploring? Disambiguating long search sessions. In *Proc. of the ACM WSDM International Conference on Web Search and Data Mining*, pages 53–62, 2014. DOI: 10.1145/2556195.2556221 87

[115] Hassan Awadallah, A., Gurrin, C., Sanderson, M., and White, R. W. Task intelligence workshop@wsdm 2019. In *Proc. of the ACM WSDM International Conference on Web Search and Data Mining*, pages 848–849, 2019. 1, 3, 8

[116] He, X., Liao, L., Zhang, H., Nie, L., Hu, X., and Chua, T.-S. Neural collaborative filtering. In *Proc. of the International Conference on the World Wide Web*, pages 173–182, 2017. DOI: 10.1145/3038912.3052569 12, 73

[117] Hersh, W., Pentecost, J., and Hickam, D. A task-oriented approach to information retrieval evaluation. *Journal of the American Society for Information Science 47*, 1:50–56, 1996. DOI: 10.1002/(sici)1097-4571(199601)47:1<50::aid-asi5>3.0.co;2-1 77

[118] Hidasi, B., Karatzoglou, A., Baltrunas, L., and Tikk, D. Session-based recommendations with recurrent neural networks. *ArXiv Preprint ArXiv:1511.06939*, 2015. 87

[119] Hienert, D., Mitsui, M., Mayr, P., Shah, C., and Belkin, N. J. The role of the task topic in web search of different task types. In *Proc. of the ACM CHIIR Conference on Human Information Interaction and Retrieval*, pages 72–81, 2018. DOI: 10.1145/3176349.3176382 29, 56

[120] Hua, S., and Wang. Identifying users' topical tasks in web search. In *Proc. of the ACM WSDM International Conference on Web Search and Data Mining*, pages 93–102, 2013. DOI: 10.1145/2433396.2433410 22

[121] Huang, J., White, R. W., Buscher, G., and Wang, K. Improving searcher models using mouse cursor activity. In *Proc. of the ACM SIGIR Conference on Research and Development in Information Retrieval*, pages 195–204, 2012. DOI: 10.1145/2348283.2348313 88

[122] Huang, M., Zhu, X., and Gao, J. Challenges in building intelligent open-domain dialog systems. *ACM Transactions on Information Systems 38*, 3:1–32, 2020. DOI: 10.1145/3383123 84

[123] Huffman, S. B. and Hochster, M. How well does result relevance predict session satisfaction? In *Proc. of the ACM SIGIR Conference on Research and Development in Information Retrieval*, pages 567–574, 2007. DOI: 10.1145/1277741.1277839 88

[124] Huurdeman, H. C. Dynamic compositions: Recombining search user interface features for supporting complex work tasks. In *Proc. of the CEUR Workshop*, 1798:22–25, 2017. 21

[125] Ingwersen, P. Cognitive perspectives of information retrieval interaction: Elements of a cognitive IR theory. *Journal of Documentation 52*, 1:3–50, 1996. DOI: 10.1108/eb026960 15

[126] Ingwersen, P. and Järvelin, K. *The Turn: Integration of Information Seeking and Retrieval in Context.* Springer, 2006. 11, 12, 50, 75

[127] Jacques, R. D. The nature of engagement and its role in hypermedia evaluation and design. Ph.D. thesis, South Bank University, 1996. 84

[128] Jansen, B. J. and Booth, D. Classifying web queries by topic and user intent. In *Proc. of the ACM SIGCHI Extended Abstracts on Human Factors in Computing Systems*, pages 4285–4290, 2010. DOI: 10.1145/1753846.1754140 33

[129] Järvelin, K., Price, S. L., Delcambre, L. M., and Nielsen, M. L. Discounted cumulated gain based evaluation of multiple-query IR sessions. In *Proc. of the European Conference on Information Retrieval*, pages 4–15, 2008. DOI: 10.1007/978-3-540-78646-7_4 82, 86

[130] Järvelin, K., Vakkari, P., Arvola, P., Baskaya, F., Järvelin, A., Kekäläinen, J., Keskustalo, H., Kumpulainen, S., Saastamoinen, M., Savolainen, R., et al. Task-based information interaction evaluation: The viewpoint of program theory. *ACM Transactions on Information Systems 33*, 1:1–30, 2015. DOI: 10.1145/2699660 75

[131] Jiang, J. and Allan, J. Adaptive effort for search evaluation metrics. In *Proc. of the European Conference on Information Retrieval*, pages 187–199, 2016. DOI: 10.1007/978-3-319-30671-1_14 82

[132] Jiang, J. and Allan, J. Correlation between system and user metrics in a session. In *Proc. of the ACM CHIIR on Conference on Human Information Interaction and Retrieval*, pages 285–288, 2016. DOI: 10.1145/2854946.2855005 88

[133] Jiang, J., Hassan Awadallah, A., Shi, X., and White, R. W. Understanding and predicting graded search satisfaction. In *Proc. of the ACM WSDM International Conference on Web Search and Data Mining*, pages 57–66, 2015. DOI: 10.1145/2684822.2685319 88

[134] Jiang, J., He, D., and Allan, J. Searching, browsing, and clicking in a search session: Changes in user behavior by task and over time. In *Proc. of the ACM SIGIR Conference on Research and Development in Information Retrieval*, pages 607–616, 2014. DOI: 10.1145/2600428.2609633 16, 51, 56

[135] John, B. E. and Kieras, D. E. The GOMS family of user interface analysis techniques: Comparison and contrast. *ACM Transactions on Computer-Human Interaction 3*, 4:320–351, 1996. DOI: 10.1145/235833.236054 81

[136] Jones, K. S. What's the value of TREC: Is there a gap to jump or a chasm to bridge? *ACM SIGIR Forum 40*, 1:10–20, 2006. DOI: 10.1145/1147197.1147198 76

[137] Jones, R. and Klinkner, K. L. Beyond the session timeout: Automatic hierarchical segmentation of search topics in query logs. In *Proc. of the ACM CIKM Conference on Information and Knowledge Management*, pages 699–708, 2008. DOI: 10.1145/1458082.1458176 22, 63, 80

[138] Jones, R., Rey, B., Madani, O., and Greiner, W. Generating query substitutions. In *Proc. of the International Conference on the World Wide Web*, pages 387–396, 2006. DOI: 10.1145/1135777.1135835 2

[139] Kahneman, D., Krueger, A. B., Schkade, D. A., Schwarz, N., and Stone, A. A. A survey method for characterizing daily life experience: The day reconstruction method. *Science 306*, 5702:1776–1780, 2004. DOI: 10.1126/science.1103572 86, 96

[140] Kahneman, D. and Tversky, A. Intuitive prediction: Biases and corrective procedures. *Technical Report*, Decisions and Designs Inc., Mclean, 1977. DOI: 10.1017/cbo9780511809477.031 82

[141] Kamar, E. and Horvitz, E. Jogger: Models for context-sensitive reminding. In *Proc. of the International Conference on Autonomous Agents and Multiagent Systems*, pages 1089–1090, 2011. 91, 102

[142] Kamps, J., Geva, S., Peters, C., Sakai, T., Trotman, A., and Voorhees, E. Report on the SIGIR 2009 workshop on the future of IR evaluation. *ACM SIGIR Forum 43*, 2:13–23, 2009. DOI: 10.1145/1670564.1670567 82

[143] Kamsin, A., Blandford, A., and Cox, A. L. Personal task management: My tools fall apart when I'm very busy! In *Proc. of the ACM SIGCHI Extended Abstracts on Human Factors in Computing Systems*, pages 1369–1374, 2012. DOI: 10.1145/2212776.2212457 102

[144] Kazai, G. and Lalmas, M. Extended cumulated gain measures for the evaluation of content-oriented XML retrieval. *ACM Transactions on Information Systems 24*, 4:503–542, 2006. DOI: 10.1145/1185877.1185883 84

[145] Kellar, M., Watters, C., and Shepherd, M. A field study characterizing web-based information-seeking tasks. *Journal of the American Society for Information Science and Technology 58*, 7:999–1018, 2007. DOI: 10.1002/asi.20590 33

[146] Kelly, D. Methods for evaluating interactive information retrieval systems with users. *Foundations and Trends in Information Retrieval 3*, 1–2:1–224, 2009. DOI: 10.1561/1500000012 2, 29, 75, 76

[147] Kelly, D. When effort exceeds expectations: A theory of search task difficulty. In *Proc. of the ECIR Workshop on Supporting Complex Search Tasks*, 2015. 82

[148] Kelly, D., Arguello, J., and Capra, R. NSF workshop on task-based information search systems. *ACM SIGIR Forum 47*, 2:116–127, 2013. DOI: 10.1145/2568388.2568407 3

[149] Kelly, D., Arguello, J., Edwards, A., and Wu, W.-C. Development and evaluation of search tasks for IIR experiments using a cognitive complexity framework. In *Proc. of the ACM ICTIR International Conference on the Theory of Information Retrieval*, pages 101–110, 2015. DOI: 10.1145/2808194.2809465 11, 20, 29, 32, 36

[150] Kelly, D. and Belkin, N. J. Display time as implicit feedback: Understanding task effects. In *Proc. of the ACM SIGIR Conference on Research and Development in Information Retrieval*, pages 377–384, 2004. DOI: 10.1145/1008992.1009057 80, 88

[151] Kelly, D. and Cool, C. The effects of topic familiarity on information search behavior. In *Proc. of the ACM/IEEE-CS JCDL Joint Conference on Digital Libraries*, pages 74–75, 2002. DOI: 10.1145/544220.544232 89

[152] Kelly, D., Dumais, S., and Pedersen, J. O. Evaluation challenges and directions for information-seeking support systems. *Computer*, 3:60–66, 2009. DOI: 10.1109/mc.2009.82 77, 87

[153] Kelly, J. D. Understanding implicit feedback and document preference: A naturalistic user study. Ph.D. thesis, Rutgers University, 2004. DOI: 10.1145/986278.986298 86, 96

[154] Kessell, A. and Chan, C. Castaway: A context-aware task management system. In *Proc. of the ACM SIGCHI Extended Abstracts on Human Factors in Computing Systems*, pages 941–946, 2006. DOI: 10.1145/1125451.1125633 102

[155] Khakurel, J., Knutas, A., Immonen, M., and Porras, J. Intended use of smartwatches and pedometers in the university environment: An empirical analysis. In *Proc. of the ACM International Joint Conference on Pervasive and Ubiquitous Computing*, pages 97–100, 2017. DOI: 10.1145/3123024.3123147 56

[156] Kim, J. The nature of engagement and its role in hypermedia evaluation and design. Ph.D. thesis, Rutgers University, 2006. 21

[157] Kim, Y., Hassan, A., White, R. W., and Zitouni, I. Modeling dwell time to predict click-level satisfaction. In *Proc. of the ACM WSDM International Conference on Web Search and Data Mining*, pages 193–202, 2014. DOI: 10.1145/2556195.2556220 88

[158] Kiseleva, J., Thanh Lam, H., Pechenizkiy, M., and Calders, T. Discovering temporal hidden contexts in web sessions for user trail prediction. In *Proc. of the International Conference on the World Wide Web*, pages 1067–1074, 2013. DOI: 10.1145/2487788.2488120 14, 101

[159] Kiseleva, J., Tuzhilin, A., Kamps, J., Mueller, M. J., Bernardi, L., Davis, C., Kovacek, I., Einarsen, M. S., and Hiemstra, D. Beyond movie recommendations: Solving the continuous cold start problem in e-commerce recommendations. *ArXiv Preprint ArXiv:1607.07904*, 2016. 102

[160] Kiseleva, J., Williams, K., Jiang, J., Hassan Awadallah, A., Crook, A. C., Zitouni, I., and Anastasakos, T. Understanding user satisfaction with intelligent assistants. In *Proc. of the ACM CHIIR Conference on Human Information Interaction and Retrieval*, pages 121–130, 2016. DOI: 10.1145/2854946.2854961 84, 88

[161] Koenemann, J. and Belkin, N. J. Case for interaction: A study of interactive information retrieval behavior and effectiveness. In *Proc. of the ACM SIGCHI Conference on Human Factors in Computing Systems*, pages 205–212, 1996. DOI: 10.1145/238386.238487 19

[162] Kohavi, R., Longbotham, R., Sommerfield, D., and Henne, R. M. Controlled experiments on the Web: Survey and practical guide. *Data Mining and Knowledge Discovery* 18, 1:140–181, 2009. DOI: 10.1007/s10618-008-0114-1 76, 98

[163] Kokkalis, N., Köhn, T., Huebner, J., Lee, M., Schulze, F., and Klemmer, S. R. Taskgenies: Automatically providing action plans helps people complete tasks. *ACM Transactions on Computer-Human Interaction 20*, 5:1–25, 2013. DOI: 10.1145/2513560 14, 101

[164] Koolen, M., Kamps, J., Bogers, T., Belkin, N., Kelly, D., and Yilmaz, E. Report on the second workshop on supporting complex search tasks. *ACM SIGIR Forum 51*, 1:58–66, 2017. DOI: 10.1145/3130332.3130343 21

[165] Kotov, A., Bennett, P. N., White, R. W., Dumais, S. T., and Teevan, J. Modeling and analysis of cross-session search tasks. In *Proc. of the ACM SIGIR Conference on Research and Development in Information Retrieval*, pages 5–14, 2011. DOI: 10.1145/2009916.2009922 22, 85

[166] Kuhlthau, C. C. Inside the search process: Information seeking from the user's perspective. *Journal of the American Society for Information Science and Technology 42*, 5:361–371, 1991. DOI: 10.1002/(sici)1097-4571(199106)42:5<361::aid-asi6>3.0.co;2-# 17, 18

[167] Kuhlthau, C. C. A principle of uncertainty for information seeking. *Journal of Documentation 49*, 4:339–355, 1993. DOI: 10.1108/eb026918 17

[168] Kuhlthau, C. C., Heinström, J., and Todd, R. J. The "information search process" revisited: Is the model still useful. *Information Research 13*, 4:13–4, 2008. 17

[169] Lagergren, E. and Over, P. Comparing interactive information retrieval systems across sites: The TREC-6 interactive track matrix experiment. In *Proc. of the ACM SIGIR Conference on Research and Development in Information Retrieval*, pages 164–172, 1998. DOI: 10.1145/290941.290986 98

[170] Lalmas, M., O'Brien, H., and Yom-Tov, E. Measuring user engagement. *Synthesis Lectures on Information Concepts, Retrieval, and Services 6*, 4:1–132, 2014. DOI: 10.2200/s00605ed1v01y201410icr038 84

[171] Lamming, M. and Flynn, M. Forget-me-not: Intimate computing in support of human memory. In *Proc. of the International Symposium on Next Generation Human Interface*, p. 4, 1994. 91

[172] Landis, J. R. and Koch, G. G. The measurement of observer agreement for categorical data. *Biometrics*, pages 159–174, 1977. DOI: 10.2307/2529310 54

[173] Larsen, B., Lioma, C., and de Vries, A. Report on TBAS 2012: Workshop on task-based and aggregated search. *ACM SIGIR Forum 46*, 1:71–77, 2012. DOI: 10.1145/2215676.2215684 7

[174] Larson, R. and Csikszentmihalyi, M. The experience sampling method. In *Flow and the Foundations of Positive Psychology*, pages 21–34, Springer, 2014. DOI: 10.1007/978-94-017-9088-8_2 86

[175] Leshed, G. and Sengers, P. I lie to myself that I have freedom in my own schedule productivity tools and experiences of busyness. In *Proc. of the ACM SIGCHI Conference on Human Factors in Computing Systems*, pages 905–914, 2011. DOI: 10.1145/1978942.1979077 102

[176] Li, J., Huffman, S., and Tokuda, A. Good abandonment in mobile and PC internet search. In *Proc. of the ACM SIGIR Conference on Research and Development in Information Retrieval*, pages 43–50, 2009. DOI: 10.1145/1571941.1571951 88

[177] Li, J., Peng, B., Lee, S., Gao, J., Takanobu, R., Zhu, Q., Huang, M., Schulz, H., Atkinson, A., and Adada, M. Results of the multi-domain task-completion dialog challenge. In *Proc. of the AAAI Dialog System Technology Challenge Workshop*, 2020. 89

[178] Li, J., Ren, P., Chen, Z., Ren, Z., Lian, T., and Ma, J. Neural attentive session-based recommendation. In *Proc. of the ACM CIKM Conference on Information and Knowledge Management*, pages 1419–1428, 2017. DOI: 10.1145/3132847.3132926 87

[179] Li, L., Deng, H., Dong, A., Chang, Y., and Zha, H. Identifying and labeling search tasks via query-based hawkes processes. In *Proc. of the ACM SIGKDD Conference on Knowledge Discovery and Data Mining*, pages 731–740, 2014. DOI: 10.1145/2623330.2623679 23

[180] Li, Y. Relationships among work tasks, search tasks, and interactive information searching behavior. Ph.D. thesis, Rutgers University, 2008. 22

[181] Li, Y. Exploring the relationships between work task and search task in information search. *Journal of the American Society for Information Science and Technology 60*, 2:275–291, 2009. DOI: 10.1002/asi.20977 14, 16

[182] Li, Y. An exploration of the relationships between work tasks and users' interaction performance. In *Proc. of the ASIS&T Annual Meeting*, pages 1–9, 2010. DOI: 10.1002/meet.14504701127 16

[183] Li, Y. and Belkin, N. J. A faceted approach to conceptualizing tasks in information seeking. *Information Processing and Management 44*, 6:1822–1837, 2008. DOI: 10.1016/j.ipm.2008.07.005 11, 16, 21, 22, 29, 49, 70

[184] Lian, J., Zhou, X., Zhang, F., Chen, Z., Xie, X., and Sun, G. xDeepFM: Combining explicit and implicit feature interactions for recommender systems. In *Proc. of the ACM SIGKDD Conference on Knowledge Discovery and Data Mining*, pages 1754–1763, 2018. DOI: 10.1145/3219819.3220023 12

[185] Liao, Z., Song, Y., He, L.-w., and Huang, Y. Evaluating the effectiveness of search task trails. In *Proc. of the International Conference on the World Wide Web*, pages 489–498, 2012. DOI: 10.1145/2187836.2187903 81, 87

[186] Lin, S.-J. and Belkin, N. J. Validation of a model of information seeking over multiple search sessions. *Journal of the American Society for Information Science and Technology 56*, 4:393–415, 2005. DOI: 10.1002/asi.20127 15

[187] Liono, J., Rahaman, M. S., Salim, F. D., Ren, Y., Spina, D., Scholer, F., Trippas, J. R., Sanderson, M., Bennett, P. N., and White, R. W. Intelligent task recognition: Towards enabling productivity assistance in daily life. In *Proc. of the International Conference on Multimedia Retrieval*, pages 472–478, 2020. DOI: 10.1145/3372278.3390703 96

[188] Liono, J., Trippas, J. R., Spina, D., Rahaman, M. S., Ren, Y., Salim, F. D., Sanderson, M., Scholer, F., and White, R. W. Building a benchmark for task progress in digital assistants. In *Proc. of the WSDM Task Intelligence Workshop*, 2019. 86

[189] Liu, C.-W., Lowe, R., Serban, I., Noseworthy, M., Charlin, L., and Pineau, J. How not to evaluate your dialogue system: An empirical study of unsupervised evaluation metrics for dialogue response generation. In *Proc. of the Conference on Empirical Methods in Natural Language Processing*, pages 2122–2132, 2016. DOI: 10.18653/v1/d16-1230 88

[190] Liu, J., Belkin, N. J., Zhang, X., and Yuan, X. Examining users' knowledge change in the task completion process. *Information Processing and Management 49*, 5:1058–1074, 2013. DOI: 10.1016/j.ipm.2012.08.006 78

[191] Liu, J., Cole, M. J., Liu, C., Bierig, R., Gwizdka, J., Belkin, N. J., Zhang, J., and Zhang, X. Search behaviors in different task types. In *Proc. of the Annual Joint Conference on Digital Libraries*, pages 69–78, 2010. DOI: 10.1145/1816123.1816134 16, 51, 56, 80

[192] Liu, J., Gwizdka, J., Liu, C., and Belkin, N. J. Predicting task difficulty for different task types. In *Proc. of the ASIS&T Annual Meeting*, pages 1–16, 2010. DOI: 10.1002/meet.14504701173 16, 56

[193] Liu, J. and Kim, C. S. Why do users perceive search tasks as difficult? Exploring difficulty in different task types. In *Proc. of the Symposium on Human-Computer Interaction and Information Retrieval*, pages 1–10, 2013. DOI: 10.1145/2528394.2528399 56

[194] Liu, J., Mitsui, M., Belkin, N. J., and Shah, C. Task, information seeking intentions, and user behavior: Toward a multi-level understanding of web search. In *Proc. of the ACM CHIIR Conference on Human Information Interaction and Retrieval*, pages 123–132, 2019. DOI: 10.1145/3295750.3298922 11, 21, 33

[195] Liu, J., Sarkar, S., and Shah, C. Identifying and predicting the states of complex search tasks. In *Proc. of the ACM CHIIR Conference on Human Information Interaction and Retrieval*, pages 193–202, 2020. DOI: 10.1145/3343413.3377976 3, 51

[196] Liu, J. and Shah, C. Proactive identification of query failure. *Proc. of the ASIS&T Annual Meeting 56*, 1:176–185, 2019. DOI: 10.1002/pra2.15 21

[197] Liu, M., Liu, Y., Mao, J., Luo, C., and Ma, S. Towards designing better session search evaluation metrics. In *Proc. of the ACM SIGIR Conference on Research and Development in Information Retrieval*, pages 1121–1124, 2018. DOI: 10.1145/3209978.3210097 88

[198] Liu, M., Mao, J., Liu, Y., Zhang, M., and Ma, S. Investigating cognitive effects in session-level search user satisfaction. In *Proc. of the ACM SIGKDD Conference on Knowledge Discovery and Data Mining*, pages 923–931, 2019. DOI: 10.1145/3292500.3330981 88

[199] Lopez, S. J. and Snyder, C. R., Eds. *The Oxford Handbook of Positive Psychology*. Oxford University Press, 2009. 88

[200] Lucchese, C., Orlando, S., Perego, R., Silvestri, F., and Tolomei, G. Modeling and predicting the task-by-task behavior of search engine users. In *Proc. of the Conference on Open Research Areas in Information Retrieval*, pages 77–84. 23

[201] Lucchese, C., Orlando, S., Perego, R., Silvestri, F., and Tolomei, G. Detecting task-based query sessions using collaborative knowledge. In *Proc. of the International Conference on Web Intelligence and Intelligent Agent Technology*, pages 128–131, 2010. DOI: 10.1109/wi-iat.2010.281 23

[202] Lucchese, C., Orlando, S., Perego, R., Silvestri, F., and Tolomei, G. Identifying task-based sessions in search engine query logs. In *Proc. of the ACM WSDM International Conference on Web Search and Data Mining*, pages 277–286, 2011. DOI: 10.1145/1935826.1935875 22, 23

[203] Lucchese, C., Orlando, S., Perego, R., Silvestri, F., and Tolomei, G. Discovering tasks from search engine query logs. *ACM Transactions on Information Systems 31*, 3, 2013. DOI: 10.1145/2493175.2493179 22, 23

[204] Ludewig, M., Mauro, N., Latifi, S., and Jannach, D. Empirical analysis of session-based recommendation algorithms. *User Modeling and User-Adapted Interaction*, pages 1–33, 2020. DOI: 10.1007/s11257-020-09277-1 87

[205] Luo, J., Wing, C., Yang, H., and Hearst, M. The water filling model and the cube test: Multi-dimensional evaluation for professional search. In *Proc. of the ACM CIKM Conference on Information and Knowledge Management*, pages 709–714, 2013. DOI: 10.1145/2505515.2523648 86

[206] Luo, J., Zhang, S., and Yang, H. Win-win search: Dual-agent stochastic game in session search. In *Proc. of the ACM SIGIR Conference on Research and Development in Information Retrieval*, pages 587–596, 2014. DOI: 10.1145/2600428.2609629 72

[207] Machmouchi, W., Awadallah, A. H., Zitouni, I., and Buscher, G. Beyond success rate: Utility as a search quality metric for online experiments. In *Proc. of the ACM CIKM Conference on Information and Knowledge Management*, pages 757–765, 2017. DOI: 10.1145/3132847.3132850 93

[208] Manning, C. D., Surdeanu, M., Bauer, J., Finkel, J. R., Bethard, S., and McClosky, D. The Stanford CoreNLP natural language processing toolkit. In *Proc. of Annual Meeting of the Association for Computational Linguistics: System Demonstrations*, pages 55–60, 2014. DOI: 10.3115/v1/p14-5010 70

[209] Marchionini, G. Information-seeking strategies of novices using a full-text electronic encyclopedia. *Journal of the American Society for Information Science and Technology 40*, 1:54–66, 1989. DOI: 10.1002/(sici)1097-4571(198901)40:1<54::aid-asi6>3.0.co;2-r 21, 56

[210] Marchionini, G. and Maurer, H. The roles of digital libraries in teaching and learning. *Communications of the ACM 38*, 4:67–75, 1995. DOI: 10.1145/205323.205345 2, 3

[211] Maynard, H. B., Stegemerten, G. J., and Schwab, J. L. *Methods–Time Measurement*. McGraw-Hill, 1948. DOI: 10.2307/2519095 81

[212] Mehrotra, R., Awadallah, A. H., Kholy, A. E., and Zitouni, I. Hey cortana! exploring the use cases of a desktop based digital assistant. In *Proc. of the SIGIR Workshop on Conversational Approaches to Information Retrieval*, 2017. 89

[213] Mehrotra, R., Awadallah, A. H., and Yilmaz, E. Learnir: WSDM 2018 workshop on learning from user interactions. In *Proc. of the ACM WSDM International Conference on Web Search and Data Mining*, pages 797–798, 2018. DOI: 10.1145/3159652.3160598 8

[214] Mehrotra, R., Bhattacharya, P., and Yilmaz, E. Characterizing users' multi-tasking behavior in web search. In *Proc. of the ACM CHIIR Conference on Human Information Interaction and Retrieval*, pages 297–300, 2016. DOI: 10.1145/2854946.2855006 23, 63

[215] Mehrotra, R., Bhattacharya, P., and Yilmaz, E. Deconstructing complex search tasks: A Bayesian nonparametric approach for extracting sub-tasks. In *Proc. of the Conference of the North American Chapter of the Association for Computational Linguistics: Human Language Technologies*, pages 599–605, 2016. DOI: 10.18653/v1/n16-1073 22, 23

[216] Mehrotra, R. and Yilmaz, E. Terms, topics and tasks: Enhanced user modelling for better personalization. In *Proc. of the ACM ICTIR International Conference on The Theory of Information Retrieval*, pages 131–140, 2015. DOI: 10.1145/2808194.2809467 23, 63

[217] Mehrotra, R. and Yilmaz, E. Towards hierarchies of search tasks and subtasks. In *Proc. of the International Conference on the World Wide Web*, pages 73–74, 2015. DOI: 10.1145/2740908.2742777 23

[218] Mehrotra, R. and Yilmaz, E. Extracting hierarchies of search tasks and subtasks via a Bayesian nonparametric approach. In *Proc. of the ACM SIGIR Conference on Research and Development in Information Retrieval*, pages 285–294, 2017. DOI: 10.1145/3077136.3080823 22, 23

[219] Mehrotra, R. and Yilmaz, E. Task embeddings: Learning query embeddings using task context. In *Proc. of the ACM CIKM Conference on Information and Knowledge Management*, pages 2199–2202, 2017. DOI: 10.1145/3132847.3133098 23

[220] Mehrotra, R., Yilmaz, E., and Verma, M. Task-based user modelling for personalization via probabilistic matrix factorization. In *RecSys Posters*, 2014. 63, 87

[221] Mishra, N., White, R. W., Ieong, S., and Horvitz, E. Time-critical search. In *Proc. of the ACM SIGIR Conference on Research and Development in Information Retrieval*, pages 747–756, 2014. DOI: 10.1145/2600428.2609613 89

[222] Mitsui, M., Liu, J., Belkin, N., and Shah, C. Predicting information seeking intentions from search behaviors. In *Proc. of the ACM SIGIR Conference on Research and Development in Information Retrieval*, pages 1121–1124, 2017. DOI: 10.1145/3077136.3080737 51, 56

[223] Mitsui, M., Liu, J., and Shah, C. Coagmento: Past, present, and future of an individual and collaborative information seeking platform. In *Proc. of the ACM CHIIR Conference on Human Information Interaction and Retrieval*, pages 325–328, 2018. DOI: 10.1145/3176349.3176896 49

[224] Mitsui, M., Liu, J., and Shah, C. How much is too much?: Whole session vs. first query behaviors in task type prediction. In *Proc. of the ACM SIGIR Conference on Research and Development in Information Retrieval*, pages 1141–1144, 2018. DOI: 10.1145/3209978.3210105 49

[225] Mitsui, M. and Shah, C. The broad view of task type using path analysis. In *Proc. of the ACM ICTIR International Conference on Theory of Information Retrieval*, pages 131–138, 2018. DOI: 10.1145/3234944.3234951 55, 57, 89

[226] Mitsui, M. and Shah, C. Bridging gaps: Predicting user and task characteristics from partial user information. In *Proc. of the ACM SIGIR Conference on Research and Development in Information Retrieval*, pages 415–424, 2019. DOI: 10.1145/3331184.3331221 3

[227] Mitsui, M., Shah, C., and Belkin, N. J. Extracting information seeking intentions for web search sessions. In *Proc. of the ACM SIGIR Conference on Research and Development in Information Retrieval*, pages 841–844, 2016. DOI: 10.1145/2911451.2914746 33, 50, 56

[228] Mizzaro, S. Relevance: The whole history. *Journal of the American Society for Information Science 48*, 9:810–832, 1997. DOI: 10.1002/(sici)1097-4571(199709)48:9<810::aid-asi6>3.0.co;2-u 86

[229] Mnih, V., Kavukcuoglu, K., Silver, D., Rusu, A. A., Veness, J., Bellemare, M. G., Graves, A., Riedmiller, M., Fidjeland, A. K., Ostrovski, G., et al. Human-level control through deep reinforcement learning. *Nature 518*, 7540:529–533, 2015. DOI: 10.1038/nature14236 71

[230] Moffat, A. Seven numeric properties of effectiveness metrics. In *Proc. of the Asia Information Retrieval Symposium*, pages 1–12, 2013. DOI: 10.1007/978-3-642-45068-6_1 89

[231] Moffat, A., Bailey, P., Scholer, F., and Thomas, P. Incorporating user expectations and behavior into the measurement of search effectiveness. *ACM Transactions on Information Systems 35*, 3:1–38, 2017. DOI: 10.1145/3052768 83, 86

[232] Moffat, A. and Zobel, J. Rank-biased precision for measurement of retrieval effectiveness. *ACM Transactions on Information Systems 27*, 1:1–27, 2008. DOI: 10.1145/1416950.1416952 82

[233] Montanez, G. D., White, R. W., and Huang, X. Cross-device search. In *Proc. of the ACM CIKM Conference on Information and Knowledge Management*, pages 1669–1678, 2014. DOI: 10.1145/2661829.2661910 85

[234] Mukherjee, S., Mukherjee, S., Hasegawa, M., Awadallah, A. H., and White, R. Smart to-do: Automatic generation of to-do items from emails. In *Proc. of the Annual Meeting of the Association for Computational Linguistics*, pages 8680–8689, 2020. DOI: 10.18653/v1/2020.acl-main.767 101

[235] Myers, K., Berry, P., Blythe, J., Conley, K., Gervasio, M., McGuinness, D. L., Morley, D., Pfeffer, A., Pollack, M., and Tambe, M. An intelligent personal assistant for task and time management. *AI Magazine 28*, 2:47–47, 2007. 3, 13, 14, 101

[236] Nouri, E., Sim, R., Fourney, A., and White, R. W. Step-wise recommendation for complex task support. In *Proc. of the ACM CHIIR Conference on Human Information Interaction and Retrieval*, pages 203–212, 2020. DOI: 10.1145/3343413.3377964 95

[237] O'Brien, H. L. and Toms, E. G. What is user engagement? A conceptual framework for defining user engagement with technology. *Journal of the American Society for Information Science and Technology 59*, 6:938–955, 2008. DOI: 10.1002/asi.20801 84, 89

[238] O'Connor, B., Krieger, M., and Ahn, D. TweetMotif: Exploratory search and topic summarization for twitter. In *Proc. of the International AAAI Conference on Web and Social Media*, 4, 2010. 64

[239] Oddy, R. N. Information retrieval through man-machine dialogue. *Journal of Documentation 33*, 1:1–14, 1977. DOI: 10.1108/eb026631 18

[240] Odijk, D., White, R. W., Hassan Awadallah, A., and Dumais, S. T. Struggling and success in web search. In *Proc. of the ACM CIKM Conference on Information and Knowledge Management*, pages 1551–1560, 2015. DOI: 10.1145/2806416.2806488 87

[241] Oliver, R. L. *Satisfaction: A Behavioral Perspective on the Consumer: A Behavioral Perspective on the Consumer*. Routledge, 2014. 88

[242] Pääkkönen, T., Kekäläinen, J., Keskustalo, H., Azzopardi, L., Maxwell, D., and Järvelin, K. Validating simulated interaction for retrieval evaluation. *Information Retrieval Journal 20*, 4:338–362, 2017. DOI: 10.1007/s10791-017-9301-2 76

[243] Pietquin, O. and Hastie, H. A survey on metrics for the evaluation of user simulations. *The Knowledge Engineering Review 28*, 1:59, 2013. DOI: 10.1017/s0269888912000343 89

[244] Pirolli, P. *Information Foraging Theory: Adaptive Interaction with Information*. Oxford University Press, 2007. 82

[245] Qiu, L. Analytical searching vs. browsing in hypertext information retrieval systems. *Canadian Journal of Information and Library Science 18*, 4:1–13, 1993. 21

[246] Radlinski, F. and Craswell, N. Comparing the sensitivity of information retrieval metrics. In *Proc. of the ACM SIGIR Conference on Research and Development in Information Retrieval*, pages 667–674, 2010. DOI: 10.1145/1835449.1835560 68

[247] Radlinski, F. and Joachims, T. Query chains: Learning to rank from implicit feedback. In *Proc. of the ACM SIGKDD Conference on Knowledge Discovery and Data Mining*, pages 239–248, 2005. DOI: 10.1145/1081870.1081899 22

[248] Radlinski, F., Szummer, M., and Craswell, N. Inferring query intent from reformulations and clicks. In *Proc. of the International Conference on the World Wide Web*, pages 1171–1172, 2010. DOI: 10.1145/1772690.1772859 22

[249] Reichheld, F. F. The one number you need to grow. *Harvard Business Review 81*, 12:46–55, 2003. 89

[250] Rha, E. Y., Mitsui, M., Belkin, N. J., and Shah, C. Exploring the relationships between search intentions and query reformulations. *Proc. of the Association for Information Science and Technology 53*, 1:1–9, 2016. DOI: 10.1002/pra2.2016.14505301048 33, 34, 56

[251] Rhodes, B. J. The wearable remembrance agent: A system for augmented memory. *Personal Technologies 1*, 4:218–224, 1997. DOI: 10.1007/bf01682024 102

[252] Rieh, S. Y., Collins-Thompson, K., Hansen, P., and Lee, H.-J. Towards searching as a learning process: A review of current perspectives and future directions. *Journal of Information Science 42*, 1:19–34, 2016. DOI: 10.1177/0165551515615841 78

[253] Robertson, S. E., Kanoulas, E., and Yilmaz, E. Extending average precision to graded relevance judgments. In *Proc. of the ACM SIGIR Conference on Research and Development in Information Retrieval*, pages 603–610, 2010. DOI: 10.1145/1835449.1835550 82

[254] Rose, D. E. and Levinson, D. Understanding user goals in web search. In *Proc. of the International Conference on the World Wide Web*, ACM, pages 13–19, 2004. DOI: 10.1145/988672.988675 33

[255] Rossi, P. H., Lipsey, M. W., and Henry, G. T. *Evaluation: A Systematic Approach*. Sage Publications, 2018. 75

[256] Rouse, W. B. and Rouse, S. H. Human information seeking and design of information systems. *Information Processing and Management 20*, 1–2:129–138, 1984. DOI: 10.1016/0306-4573(84)90044-x 18

[257] Rowley, J. Product search in e-shopping: A review and research propositions. *Journal of Consumer Marketing 17*, 1:20–35, 2000. DOI: 10.1108/07363760010309528 71

[258] Russell, D. M., Tang, D., Kellar, M., and Jeffries, R. Task behaviors during web search: The difficulty of assigning labels. In *Proc. of the Hawaii International Conference on System Sciences*, pages 1–5, 2009. 96

[259] Saastamoinen, M. and Järvelin, K. Search task features in work tasks of varying types and complexity. *Journal of the Association for Information Science and Technology 68*, 5:1111–1123, 2017. DOI: 10.1002/asi.23766 11

[260] Sakai, T. Evaluating evaluation metrics based on the bootstrap. In *Proc. of the ACM SIGIR Conference on Research and Development in Information Retrieval*, pages 525–532, 2006. DOI: 10.1145/1148170.1148261 86

[261] Sakai, T.   Evaluation with informational and navigational intents.   In *Proc. of the International Conference on the World Wide Web*, pages 499–508, 2012. DOI: 10.1145/2187836.2187904 89

[262] Sakai, T. and Dou, Z.   Summaries, ranked retrieval and sessions: A unified framework for information access evaluation.   In *Proc. of the ACM SIGIR Conference on Research and Development in Information Retrieval*, pages 473–482, 2013. DOI: 10.1145/2484028.2484031 84

[263] Salton, G. and Buckley, C.   Improving retrieval performance by relevance feedback. *Journal of the American Society for Information Science 41*, 4:288–297, 1990. DOI: 10.1002/(sici)1097-4571(199006)41:4<288::aid-asi8>3.0.co;2-h 18

[264] Sanderson, M. Test collection based evaluation of information retrieval systems. *Foundations and Trends in Information Retrieval 4*, 4:247–375, 2010. DOI: 10.1561/1500000009 76

[265] Saracevic, T. Relevance: A review of the literature and a framework for thinking on the notion in information science. Part III: Behavior and effects of relevance. *Journal of the American Society for Information Science and Technology 58*, 13:2126–2144, 2007. DOI: 10.1002/asi.20681 87

[266] Sarkar, S., Wang, Y., and Shah, C. Investigating relations of information seeking outcomes to the selection and use of information sources. In *Proc. of the ASIS&T Annual Meeting*, pages 347–356, 2017. DOI: 10.1002/pra2.2017.14505401038 26

[267] Sarkar, S., Mitsui, M., Liu, J., and Shah, C. Implicit information need as explicit problems, help, and behavioral signals. *Information Processing and Management*, 102069, 2019. DOI: 10.1016/j.ipm.2019.102069 21, 51

[268] Savolainen, R.   Expectancy-value beliefs and information needs as motivators for task-based information seeking. *Journal of Documentation 68*, 4:492–511, 2012. DOI: 10.1108/00220411211239075 11

[269] Savolainen, R. and Kari, J. Facing and bridging gaps in web searching. *Information Processing and Management 42*, 2:519–537, 2006. DOI: 10.1016/j.ipm.2005.01.009 33

[270] Schafer, J. B., Frankowski, D., Herlocker, J., and Sen, S. Collaborative filtering recommender systems. In *The Adaptive Web*, pages 291–324, 2007. DOI: 10.1007/978-3-540-72079-9_9 12

[271] Schuth, A., Balog, K., and Kelly, L. Overview of the living labs for information retrieval evaluation (ll4ir) clef lab 2015. In *Proc. of the International Conference of the Cross-language Evaluation Forum for European Languages*, pages 484–496, 2015. 77

[272] Segerståhl, K. Crossmedia systems constructed around human activities: A field study and implications for design. In *Proc. of the IFIP Conference on Human-Computer Interaction*, pages 354–367, 2009. DOI: 10.1007/978-3-642-03658-3_41 94

[273] Shah, C. Working in collaboration-what, why, and how. In *Proc. of Collaborative Information Retrieval Workshop at CSCW 2010*, Citeseer, 2010. 75

[274] Shah, C. *Collaborative Information Seeking: The Art and Science of Making the Whole Greater than the Sum of All*. Springer, 2012. DOI: 10.1007/978-3-642-28813-5 139

[275] Shah, C. *Social Information Seeking*. Springer, 2017. DOI: 10.1007/978-3-319-56756-3 75, 139

[276] Shah, C. Information fostering-being proactive with information seeking and retrieval: Perspective paper. In *Proc. of the ACM CHIIR Conference on Human Information Interaction and Retrieval*, pages 62–71, 2018. DOI: 10.1145/3176349.3176389 66

[277] Shah, C. *A Hands-on Introduction to Data Science*. Cambridge University Press, 2020. DOI: 10.1017/9781108560412 139

[278] Shah, C., Capra, R., and Hansen, P. Collaborative information seeking [guest editors' introduction]. *Computer 47*, 3:22–25, 2014. DOI: 10.1109/mc.2014.54 139

[279] Shah, C. and White, R. W. Tutorial on task-based search and assistance. In *Proc. of the ACM SIGIR Conference on Research and Development in Information Retrieval*, pages 2436–2439, 2020. DOI: 10.1145/3397271.3401422 8

[280] Shah, C. and White, R. W. Bridging task expressions and search queries. In *Proc. of the ACM CHIIR Conference on Human Information Interaction and Retrieval*, pages 319–323, 2021. DOI: 10.1145/3406522.3446045 43, 101

[281] Shani, G. and Gunawardana, A. Evaluating recommendation systems. In *Recommender Systems Handbook*, F. Ricci, L. Rokach, and B. Shapira, Eds., pages 257–297, Springer, 2011. DOI: 10.1007/978-0-387-85820-3_8 79

[282] Shen, D., Sun, J.-T., Yang, Q., and Chen, Z. Building bridges for web query classification. In *Proc. of the ACM SIGIR Conference on Research and Development in Information Retrieval*, pages 131–138, 2006. DOI: 10.1145/1148170.1148196 22

[283] Shi, Y., Karatzoglou, A., Baltrunas, L., Larson, M., and Hanjalic, A. Cars2: Learning context-aware representations for context-aware recommendations. In *Proc. of the ACM CIKM Conference on Information and Knowledge Management*, pages 291–300, 2014. DOI: 10.1145/2661829.2662070 101

[284] Shneiderman, B. Creating creativity: User interfaces for supporting innovation. *ACM Transactions on Computer-Human Interaction 7*, 1:114–138, 2000. DOI: 10.1145/344949.345077 79

[285] Shu, K., Mukherjee, S., Zheng, G., Awadallah, A. H., Shokouhi, M., and Dumais, S. Learning with weak supervision for email intent detection. In *Proc. of the ACM SIGIR Conference on Research and Development in Information Retrieval*, pages 1051–1060, 2020. DOI: 10.1145/3397271.3401121 96

[286] Singla, A., White, R., and Huang, J. Studying trailfinding algorithms for enhanced web search. In *Proc. of the ACM SIGIR Conference on Research and Development in Information Retrieval*, pages 443–450, 2010. DOI: 10.1145/1835449.1835524 87, 101, 102

[287] Smith, C. L. and Rieh, S. Y. Knowledge-context in search systems: Toward information-literate actions. In *Proc. of the ACM CHIIR Conference on Human Information Interaction and Retrieval*, pages 55–62, 2019. DOI: 10.1145/3295750.3298940 15

[288] Smucker, M. D. and Clarke, C. L. Time-based calibration of effectiveness measures. In *Proc. of the ACM SIGIR Conference on Research and Development in Information Retrieval*, pages 95–104, 2012. DOI: 10.1145/2348283.2348300 80, 81, 84

[289] Soltani, D., Mitsui, M., and Shah, C. Coagmento v3.0: Rapid prototyping of web search experiments. In *Proc. of the ACM CHIIR Conference on Human Information Interaction and Retrieval*, pages 367–371, 2019. DOI: 10.1145/3295750.3298917 49

[290] Song, Y. and Guo, Q. Query-less: Predicting task repetition for nextgen proactive search and recommendation engines. In *Proc. of the International Conference on the World Wide Web*, pages 543–553, 2016. DOI: 10.1145/2872427.2883020 64

[291] Sormunen, E., Tanni, M., Alamettälä, T., and Heinström, J. Students' group work strategies in source-based writing assignments. *Journal of the Association for Information Science and Technology 65*, 6:1217–1231, 2014. DOI: 10.1002/asi.23032 98

[292] Spink, A. Study of interactive feedback during mediated information retrieval. *Journal of the American Society for Information Science 48*, 5:382–394, 1997. DOI: 10.1002/(sici)1097-4571(199705)48:5<382::aid-asi2>3.0.co;2-r 18

[293] Spink, A., Park, M., Jansen, B. J., and Pedersen, J. Multitasking during web search sessions. *Information Processing and Management 42*, 1:264–275, 2006. DOI: 10.1016/j.ipm.2004.10.004 81

[294] Stamou, S. and Efthimiadis, E. N. Interpreting user inactivity on search results. In *Proc. of the European Conference on Information Retrieval*, pages 100–113, 2010. DOI: 10.1007/978-3-642-12275-0_12 88

[295] Stone, S. Humanities scholars: Information needs and uses. *Journal of Documentation 38*, 4:292–313, 1982. DOI: 10.1108/eb026734 18

[296] Stumpf, S., Bao, X., Dragunov, A., Dietterich, T. G., Herlocker, J., Johnsrude, K., Li, L., and Shen, J. Predicting user tasks: I know what you're doing. In *Proc. of the AAAI Workshop on Human Comprehensible Machine Learning*, 2005. 14, 101

[297] Stumpf, S., Burnett, M., Pipek, V., and Wong, W.-K. End-user interactions with intelligent and autonomous systems. In *Proc. of the ACM SIGCHI Extended Abstracts on Human Factors in Computing Systems*, pages 2755–2758, 2012. DOI: 10.1145/2212776.2212713 7

[298] Sutton, R. S. and Barto, A. G. *Reinforcement Learning: An Introduction*. MIT Press, 2017. DOI: 10.1109/tnn.1998.712192 67, 71

[299] Tague-Sutcliffe, J. Measuring the informativeness of a retrieval process. In *Proc. of the ACM SIGIR Conference on Research and Development in Information Retrieval*, pages 23–36, 1992. DOI: 10.1145/133160.133171 89

[300] Takanobu, R., Zhu, H., and Huang, M. Guided dialog policy learning: Reward estimation for multi-domain task-oriented dialog. In *Proc. of the Conference on Empirical Methods in Natural Language Processing and the International Joint Conference on Natural Language Processing*, pages 100–110, 2019. DOI: 10.18653/v1/d19-1010 89

[301] Takanobu, R., Zhu, Q., Li, J., Peng, B., Gao, J., and Huang, M. Is your goal-oriented dialog model performing really well? Empirical analysis of system-wise evaluation. In *Proc. of the Annual Meeting of the Special Interest Group on Discourse and Dialogue*, pages 297–310, 2020. 89

[302] Taylor, A. R., Cool, C., Belkin, N. J., and Amadio, W. J. Relationships between categories of relevance criteria and stage in task completion. *Information Processing and Management 43*, 4:1071–1084, 2007. DOI: 10.1016/j.ipm.2006.09.008 86

[303] Thomas, K., Handley, S., and Newstead, S. The effects of prior experience on estimating the duration of simple tasks. *Current Psychology of Cognition 22*, 2:83–100, 2004. 82

[304] Tolomei, G., Orlando, S., and Silvestri, F. Towards task-based search and recommender systems. In *Proc. of the IEEE International Conference on Data Engineering Workshops*, pages 333–336, 2010. DOI: 10.1109/ICDEW.2010.5452726 63, 101

[305] Toms, E., MacKenzie, T., Jordan, C., O'Brien, H., Freund, L., Toze, S., Dawe, E., and MacNutt, A. How task affects information search. In *Workshop Pre-proceedings in Initiative for the Evaluation of XML Retrieval*, pages 337–341, 2007. 21

[306] Toms, E. and O'Brien, H. The ISSS measurement dilemma. *IEEE Computer 42*, 3:48, 2009. 76, 79, 88, 89

[307] Toms, E. G. Task-based information searching and retrieval. In *Interactive Information Seeking, Behaviour and Retrieval*, I. Ruthven and D. Kelly, Eds., pages 43–60, Facet, 2011. DOI: 10.29085/9781856049740.005 2

[308] Toms, E. G., O'Brien, H. L., Kopak, R., and Freund, L. Searching for relevance in the relevance of search. In *Proc. of the International Conference on Conceptions of Library and Information Sciences*, pages 59–78, 2005. DOI: 10.1007/11495222_7 89

[309] Turpin, A. and Scholer, F. User performance versus precision measures for simple search tasks. In *Proc. of the ACM SIGIR Conference on Research and Development in Information Retrieval*, pages 11–18, 2006. DOI: 10.1145/1148170.1148176 89

[310] Vakkari, P. Task complexity, problem structure and information actions: Integrating studies on information seeking and retrieval. *Information Processing and Management 35*, 6:819–837, 1999. DOI: 10.1016/S0306-4573(99)00028-X 11, 90

[311] Vakkari, P. A theory of the task-based information retrieval process: A summary and generalisation of a longitudinal study. *Journal of Documentation 57*, 1, 2001. DOI: 10.1108/eum0000000007075 3, 11, 19, 85

[312] Vakkari, P. Task-based information searching. *Annual Review of Information Science and Technology 37*, 1:413–464, 2003. DOI: 10.1002/aris.1440370110 2, 22

[313] Van Gysel, C., de Rijke, M., and Kanoulas, E. Learning latent vector spaces for product search. In *Proc. of the ACM CIKM Conference on Information and Knowledge Management*, pages 165–174, 2016. DOI: 10.1145/2983323.2983702 71

[314] Van Gysel, C., Mitra, B., Venanzi, M., Rosemarin, R., Kukla, G., Grudzien, P., and Cancedda, N. Reply with: Proactive recommendation of email attachments. In *Proc. of the ACM CIKM Conference on Information and Knowledge Management*, pages 327–336, 2017. DOI: 10.1145/3132847.3132979 71

[315] Van Meteren, R. and Van Someren, M. Using content-based filtering for recommendation. In *Proc. of the Workshop on Machine Learning in the New Information Age*, pages 47–56, 2000. 12

[316] Verberne, S., Sappelli, M., Järvelin, K., and Kraaij, W. User simulations for interactive search: Evaluating personalized query suggestion. In *Proc. of the European Conference on Information Retrieval*, pages 678–690, 2015. DOI: 10.1007/978-3-319-16354-3_75 76

[317] Verma, M. and Yilmaz, E. Entity oriented task extraction from query logs. In *Proc. of the ACM CIKM Conference on Information and Knowledge Management*, pages 1975–1978, 2014. DOI: 10.1145/2661829.2662076 23

[318] Voorhees, E. M. and Harman, D. K., Eds. *TREC: Experiment and Evaluation in Information Retrieval*. MIT Press, Cambridge, 2005. 76

[319] Vtyurina, A. and Fourney, A. Exploring the role of conversational cues in guided task support with virtual assistants. In *Proc. of the ACM SIGCHI Conference on Human Factors in Computing Systems*, pages 1–7, 2018. DOI: 10.1145/3173574.3173782 14

[320] Vu, T., Willis, A., Tran, S. N., and Song, D. Temporal latent topic user profiles for search personalisation. In *Proc. of the European Conference on Information Retrieval*, pages 605–616, 2015. DOI: 10.1007/978-3-319-16354-3_67 63

[321] Walker, M., Litman, D., Kamm, C. A., and Abella, A. Paradise: A framework for evaluating spoken dialogue agents. In *Proc. of the Annual Meeting of the Association for Computational Linguistics and Conference of the European Chapter of the Association for Computational Linguistics*, pages 271–280, 1997. DOI: 10.3115/979617.979652 89

[322] Wang, H., Song, Y., Chang, M.-W., He, X., Awadallah, A. H., and White, R. W. Modeling action-level satisfaction for search task satisfaction prediction. In *Proc. of the ACM SIGIR Conference on Research and Development in Information Retrieval*, pages 123–132, 2014. DOI: 10.1145/2600428.2609607 63

[323] Wang, H., Song, Y., Chang, M.-W., He, X., White, R. W., and Chu, W. Learning to extract cross-session search tasks. In *Proc. of the International Conference on the World Wide Web*, pages 1353–1364, 2013. DOI: 10.1145/2488388.2488507 22, 23

[324] Wang, H., Wang, N., and Yeung, D.-Y. Collaborative deep learning for recommender systems. In *Proc. of the ACM SIGKDD Conference on Knowledge Discovery and Data Mining*, pages 1235–1244, 2015. DOI: 10.1145/2783258.2783273 73

[325] Wang, H., Zhang, F., Wang, J., Zhao, M., Li, W., Xie, X., and Guo, M. RippleNet: Propagating user preferences on the knowledge graph for recommender systems. In *Proc. of the ACM CIKM Conference on Information and Knowledge Management*, pages 417–426, 2018. DOI: 10.1145/3269206.3271739 12

[326] Wang, H. J., Moshchuk, A., Gamon, M., Iqbal, S., Brown, E. T., Kapoor, A., Meek, C., Chen, E., Tian, Y., Teevan, J., et al. The activity platform. In *Proc. of the Workshop on Hot Topics in Operating Systems*, 2015. 101

[327] Wang, W., Hosseini, S., Awadallah, A. H., Bennett, P. N., and Quirk, C. Context-aware intent identification in email conversations. In *Proc. of the ACM SIGIR Conference on Research and Development in Information Retrieval*, pages 585–594, 2019. DOI: 10.1145/3331184.3331260 101

[328] Wang, Y., Huang, X., and White, R. W. Characterizing and supporting cross-device search tasks. In *Proc. of the ACM WSDM International Conference on Web Search and Data Mining*, pages 707–716, 2013. DOI: 10.1145/2433396.2433484 85

[329] Wang, Y., Sarkar, S., and Shah, C. Juggling with information sources, task type, and information quality. In *Proc. of the ACM CHIIR Conference on Human Information Interaction and Retrieval*, pages 82–91, 2018. DOI: 10.1145/3176349.3176390 27

[330] Wang, Y. and Shah, C. Exploring support for the unconquerable barriers in information seeking. In *Proc. of the ASIS&T Annual Meeting*, pages 1–5, 2016. DOI: 10.1002/pra2.2016.14505301106 26

[331] Weiser, M. The computer for the 21st century. *ACM SIGMOBILE Mobile Computing and Communications Review 3*, 3:3–11, 1999. DOI: 10.1145/329124.329126 94

[332] White, R. W. *Interactions with Search Systems*. Cambridge University Press, 2016. DOI: 10.1017/cbo9781139525305 1, 84, 140

[333] White, R. W. Opportunities and challenges in search interaction. *Communications of the ACM 61*, 12:36–38, 2018. DOI: 10.1145/3195180 88, 101

[334] White, R. W. Skill discovery in virtual assistants. *Communications of the ACM 61*, 11:106–113, 2018. DOI: 10.1145/3185336 13, 92, 93

[335] White, R. W., Bailey, P., and Chen, L. Predicting user interests from contextual information. In *Proc. of the ACM SIGIR Conference on Research and Development in Information Retrieval*, pages 363–370, 2009. DOI: 10.1145/1571941.1572005 101

[336] White, R. W., Bennett, P. N., and Dumais, S. T. Predicting short-term interests using activity-based search context. In *Proc. of the ACM CIKM Conference on Information and Knowledge Management*, pages 1009–1018, 2010. DOI: 10.1145/1871437.1871565 22, 64, 92

[337] White, R. W., Bilenko, M., and Cucerzan, S. Studying the use of popular destinations to enhance web search interaction. In *Proc. of the ACM SIGIR Conference on Research and Development in Information Retrieval*, pages 159–166, 2007. DOI: 10.1145/1277741.1277771 85, 87

[338] White, R. W., Chu, W., Hassan, A., He, X., Song, Y., and Wang, H. Enhancing personalized search by mining and modeling task behavior. In *Proc. of the International Conference on the World Wide Web*, pages 1411–1420, 2013. DOI: 10.1145/2488388.2488511 63, 87, 93

[339] White, R. W., Dumais, S. T., and Teevan, J. Characterizing the influence of domain expertise on web search behavior. In *Proc. of the ACM WSDM International Conference on Web Search and Data Mining*, pages 132–141, 2009. DOI: 10.1145/1498759.1498819 89

[340] White, R. W., Fourney, A., Herring, A., Bennett, P. N., Chandrasekaran, N., Sim, R., Nouri, E., and Encarnación, M. J. Multi-device digital assistance. *Communications of the ACM 62*, 10:28–31, 2019. DOI: 10.1145/3357159 93, 94, 95

[341] White, R. W. and Hassan Awadallah, A. Task duration estimation. In *Proc. of the ACM WSDM International Conference on Web Search and Data Mining*, pages 636–644, 2019. DOI: 10.1145/3289600.3290997 13, 14, 63, 82

[342] White, R. W., Hassan Awadallah, A., and Sim, R. Task completion detection: A study in the context of intelligent systems. In *Proc. of the ACM SIGIR Conference on Research and Development in Information Retrieval*, pages 405–414, 2019. DOI: 10.1145/3331184.3331187 13, 85, 91

[343] White, R. W. and Huang, J. Assessing the scenic route: Measuring the value of search trails in web logs. In *Proc. of the ACM SIGIR Conference on Research and Development in Information Retrieval*, pages 587–594, 2010. DOI: 10.1145/1835449.1835548 85

[344] White, R. W., Jose, J. M., van Rijsbergen, C. J., and Ruthven, I. A simulated study of implicit feedback models. In *Proc. of the European Conference on Information Retrieval*, pages 311–326, 2004. DOI: 10.1007/978-3-540-24752-4_23 76

[345] White, R. W., Kapoor, A., and Dumais, S. T. Modeling long-term search engine usage. In *Proc. of the International Conference on User Modeling, Adaptation, and Personalization*, pages 28–39, 2010. DOI: 10.1007/978-3-642-13470-8_5 79

[346] White, R. W. and Kelly, D. A study on the effects of personalization and task information on implicit feedback performance. In *Proc. of the ACM CIKM Conference on Information and Knowledge Management*, pages 297–306, 2006. DOI: 10.1145/1183614.1183659 64, 80, 88

[347] White, R. W., Nouri, E., Woffinden-Luey, J., Encarnación, M., and Jauhar, S. K. Microtask detection. *ACM Transactions on Information Systems 39*, 2:1–29, 2021. DOI: 10.1145/3432290 13, 48, 82

[348] Wildemuth, B. M. The effects of domain knowledge on search tactic formulation. *Journal of the American Society for Information Science and Technology 55*, 3:246–258, 2004. DOI: 10.1002/asi.10367 16

[349] Wildemuth, B. M. and Freund, L. Search tasks and their role in studies of search behaviors. In *Proc. of the Workshop on Human Computer Interaction and Information Retrieval*, 2009. 98

[350] Wildemuth, B. M. and Freund, L. Assigning search tasks designed to elicit exploratory search behaviors. In *Proc. of the Symposium on Human-Computer Interaction and Information Retrieval*, pages 1–10, 2012. DOI: 10.1145/2391224.2391228 26

[351] Wildemuth, B. M., Freund, L., and Toms, E. G. Studies of search task complexity or difficulty. *Science and Technology 62*, 9:1676–1695, 2014. 89

[352] Wilson, M. L., Schraefel, M., and White, R. W. Evaluating advanced search interfaces using established information-seeking models. *Journal of the American Society for Information Science and Technology 60*, 7:1407–1422, 2009. DOI: 10.1002/asi.21080 98

[353] Wilson, T. D. Models in information behaviour research. *Journal of Documentation 55*, 3:249–270, 1999. DOI: 10.1108/eum0000000007145 17

[354] Xie, H. Planned and situated aspects in interactive IR: Patterns of user interactive intentions and information seeking strategies. In *Proc. of the ASIS&T Annual Meeting*, 34:101–110, 1997. 2

[355] Xie, H. Patterns between interactive intentions and information-seeking strategies. *Information Processing and Management 38*, 1:55–77, 2002. DOI: 10.1016/s0306-4573(01)00018-8 33, 34

[356] Xie, I. *Interactive Information Retrieval in Digital Environments*. IGI Global, 2008. DOI: 10.4018/978-1-59904-240-4 15

[357] Xu, Y. and Mease, D. Evaluating web search using task completion time. In *Proc. of the ACM SIGIR Conference on Research and Development in Information Retrieval*, pages 676–677, 2009. DOI: 10.1145/1571941.1572073 80

[358] Yan, J., Chu, W., and White, R. W. Cohort modeling for enhanced personalized search. In *Proc. of the ACM SIGIR Conference on Research and Development in Information Retrieval*, pages 505–514, 2014. DOI: 10.1145/2600428.2609617 93

[359] Yang, G. H. and Soboroff, I. TREC 2016 dynamic domain track overview. In *Proc. of the Text Retrieval Conference*, 2016. 87

[360] Yao, L., Sheng, Q. Z., Qin, Y., Wang, X., Shemshadi, A., and He, Q. Context-aware point-of-interest recommendation using tensor factorization with social regularization. In *Proc. of the ACM SIGIR Conference on Research and Development in Information Retrieval*, pages 1007–1010, 2015. DOI: 10.1145/2766462.2767794 101

[361] Yilmaz, E., Verma, M., Craswell, N., Radlinski, F., and Bailey, P. Relevance and effort: An analysis of document utility. In *Proc. of the ACM CIKM Conference on Information and Knowledge Management*, pages 91–100, 2014. DOI: 10.1145/2661829.2661953 79

[362] Yilmaz, E., Verma, M., Mehrotra, R., Kanoulas, E., Carterette, B., and Craswell, N. Overview of the TREC 2015 tasks track. In *Proc. of the Text Retrieval Conference*, 2015. 76

[363] Yuan, X. and Belkin, N. J. Investigating information retrieval support techniques for different information-seeking strategies. *Journal of the American Society for Information Science and Technology 61*, 8:1543–1563, 2010. DOI: 10.1002/asi.21314 79

[364] Yuan, X. and White, R. Building the trail best traveled: Effects of domain knowledge on web search trailblazing. In *Proc. of the ACM SIGCHI Conference on Human Factors in Computing Systems*, pages 1795–1804, 2012. DOI: 10.1145/2207676.2208312 102

[365] Zakay, D. and Block, R. A. The role of attention in time estimation processes. In *Advances in Psychology*, 115:143–164, 1996. DOI: 10.1016/s0166-4115(96)80057-4 82

[366] Zamani, H. and Croft, W. B. Learning a joint search and recommendation model from user-item interactions. In *Proc. of the ACM WSDM International Conference on Web Search and Data Mining*, pages 717–725, 2020. DOI: 10.1145/3336191.3371818 70, 71, 73

[367] Zeng, C., Wang, Q., Mokhtari, S., and Li, T. Online context-aware recommendation with time varying multi-armed bandit. In *Proc. of the ACM SIGKDD Conference on Knowledge Discovery and Data Mining*, pages 2025–2034, 2016. DOI: 10.1145/2939672.2939878 101

[368] Zhang, F., Mao, J., Liu, Y., Ma, W., Zhang, M., and Ma, S. Cascade or recency: Constructing better evaluation metrics for session search. In *Proc. of the ACM SIGIR Conference on Research and Development in Information Retrieval*, pages 389–398, 2020. DOI: 10.1145/3397271.3401163 88

[369] Zhang, X., Liu, J., and Cole, M. Task topic knowledge vs. background domain knowledge: Impact of two types of knowledge on user search performance. In *Advances in Information Systems and Technologies*, pages 179–191, 2013. DOI: 10.1007/978-3-642-36981-0_17 29

[370] Zhang, X., Liu, J., Cole, M., and Belkin, N.   Predicting users' domain knowledge in information retrieval using multiple regression analysis of search behaviors. *Journal of the Association for Information Science and Technology 66*, 5:980–1000, 2015. DOI: 10.1002/asi.23218 71

[371] Zhang, Y., Zhang, J., Lease, M., and Gwizdka, J.   Multidimensional relevance modeling via psychometrics and crowdsourcing.   In *Proc. of the ACM SIGIR Conference on Research and Development in Information Retrieval*, pages 435–444, 2014. DOI: 10.1145/2600428.2609577 56

[372] Zhang, Y., Zhang, M., Liu, Y., Tat-Seng, C., Zhang, Y., and Ma, S.   Task-based recommendation on a web-scale. In *Proc. of the IEEE International Conference on Big Data*, pages 827–836, 2015. DOI: 10.1109/bigdata.2015.7363829 63, 87

[373] Zhao, X., Zhang, L., Xia, L., Ding, Z., Yin, D., and Tang, J.   Deep reinforcement learning for list-wise recommendations. *ArXiv Preprint ArXiv:1801.00209*, 2017. DOI: 10.1145/3240323.3240374 72

[374] Zheng, G., Zhang, F., Zheng, Z., Xiang, Y., Yuan, N. J., Xie, X., and Li, Z. DRN: A deep reinforcement learning framework for news recommendation. In *Proc. of the International Conference on the World Wide Web*, pages 167–176, 2018. DOI: 10.1145/3178876.3185994 13

Authors' Biographies

CHIRAG SHAH

Chirag Shah is an Associate Professor in the Information School (iSchool) at the University of Washington (UW) in Seattle. Before UW, he was on the faculty at Rutgers University. His research interests include studies of interactive information retrieval/seeking, trying to understand the task a person is doing and providing proactive recommendations. In addition, he works to make these smart systems also fair, equitable, and transparent under the umbrella of Responsible AI. Dr. Shah received his Ph.D. in Information Science from University of North Carolina (UNC) at Chapel Hill. He directs the InfoSeeking Lab where he investigates issues related to information seeking, human–computer interaction (HCI), and fairness in machine learning. Shah has authored/edited two books on Collaborative Information Seeking (CIS) [107, 274], and a book on Social Information Seeking (SIS) [275]. He was a guest editor for the *IEEE Computer Special Issue on CIS* published in March 2014 [278]. He has also written a textbook on Data Science [277]. He has taught undergraduate and graduate courses in IR, HCI, and Data Science at the University of North Carolina (UNC) Chapel Hill, Rutgers University, and University of Washington. He has also taught several courses and tutorials on topics related to search, recommendation, and fairness in machine learning at different international places, including at SIGIR, WSDM, and RecSys conferences, Russian Summer School on Information Retrieval (RuSSIR), and Asian Summer School in Information Access (ASSIA). In 2019, Shah received the Microsoft BCS/BCS IRSG Karen Spärck Jones Award for contributions to information retrieval. He is the Founding Editor-in-Chief of *ASIS&T Information Matters*.

RYEN W. WHITE

Ryen W. White is a Partner Research Area Manager at Microsoft Research, where he leads several world-class teams of scientists and engineers comprising the Language and Intelligent Assistance research area. In recent roles, Ryen led the applied science organization for Microsoft Cortana and was chief scientist for Microsoft Health. Ryen's research has historically been focused on understanding search interaction and developing tools to help people search more effectively. He received his Ph.D. in Computer Science from University of Glasgow, United Kingdom. Ryen has published hundreds of conference papers and journal articles in web search and other areas. He was identified as the "Center of the SIGIR Universe" (most central author in the co-authorship graph) in the 40 years of the ACM SIGIR conference. Ryen has received many best-paper awards in conferences and journals, including three best papers at the ACM SIGIR conference. His book, *Interactions with Search Systems* [332], received the ASIS&T Best Information Science book award in 2017. Ryen's doctoral research received the British Computer Society's Distinguished Dissertation Award. In 2014, he received the Microsoft BCS/BCS IRSG Karen Spärck Jones Award for contributions to information retrieval. Ryen co-founded the ACM SIGIR Conference on Human-Information Interaction and Retrieval (CHIIR) and chaired its inaugural steering committee. He was program chair of SIGIR 2017 and The Web Conference 2019. Ryen was co-editor-in-chief of the *Information Retrieval Journal* (2018–2021), and is now the editor-in-chief of *ACM Transactions on the Web*.

Printed in the United States
by Baker & Taylor Publisher Services